Lovescaping

Building the Humanity of Tomorrow by

Practicing Love in Action

Irene Greaves

Illustrations by Domingo Oropeza

To all my fellow human beings, in hopes that we can Lovescape together

Contents

What is your dream job?

Answering this question has always been a challenge for me. Not because I haven't known what I wanted to do with my life, but because what I wanted to do – what I wanted to be – doesn't exist in the form of a job *per se*. I have kept the answer to this question mostly to myself until now. You see, even though I've felt a pressing desire to share my message, I've been hesitant to put it into words, since its existence depends solely on actions. But I've learned that in order to discuss and pursue a dream we have to name it.

My dream job is to love.

There, I've said it; I've named it, and now I can pursue it. Lovescaping is the work of my life, my dream job. What I want to do is love and teach how to love.

What I am is a Lovescaper.

Introduction

"Contemplating death has always been a subject that leads me back to love"

bell hooks

How did this story come to be? *Lovescaping* is the story of my life, based on my experiences to date during my short time here on Earth. Even though love has been at the center of my life from the moment I was born, it wasn't until a few years ago that I had my eureka moment and realized that love is the answer. *The answer to what?* you may ask. In the pages that follow, I hope to answer that question and to propose a philosophy of life based on practicing love in action. I have been fortunate enough to have received an abundance of love from my family, my friends and my community; and this love has given me the tools to succeed in loving myself and others.

Where and how do we learn to love? Whose job is it to teach us how to love? These questions are so uncommon that we may even find them uncomfortable or superfluous. We assume that we will "pick up" love at home, through our families. However, not everyone has the privilege of learning to love from their families, and many parents--even with the best intentions--are not equipped with the tools to teach their children how to love, because they themselves never learned. And so the cycle continues, and we create a society that is love-deprived.

If you read bell hooks' quote above, perhaps you are thinking that it's strange to start with death in a book about love. But it isn't. Understanding that death is an intrinsic part of life has been an unveiling for me. I have learned to understand that the nature of life includes death: every single living organism on this planet goes through a cyclical process where there is a beginning and an end. When you look closer you will realize that they are inextricably linked, that there is no life without death, and no death without life.

Coming to terms with this obvious realization changes your perspective on death, and on life. My journey has been to make peace with death, as if death were an enemy. I used to feel anger towards death--how dare it come and take loved ones from me?

But that line of thought only led to another conclusion: I should then feel anger towards life as well. It didn't make sense to condemn death and not life. When I learned to embrace death as a natural and intrinsic part of life, it led me to love. For love is the thread that weaves together the cycle of life and death.

What do we leave behind when we die? Our bodies become ashes, dust, nutrients for other species. But what intangible things do we leave behind? What can outlive us? Only the actions we carry out in the world live on, the impact of which, depending on their magnitude, can affect those in our immediate surroundings or billions of people around the world. There is no greater impact than that of love. The only thing that can transcend our physical being is love.

The effects of love remain throughout time; love's influence can cause a ripple effect that touches and nurtures others, even long after our mortal bodies have ceased to exist. When I contemplate the death of my loved ones, I am inevitably transported to love, because love is what they leave behind.

Before articulating the philosophy of Lovescaping, the best way I could find to define love was through friendship. Ever since I left my home country, Venezuela, in 2005, I have been living in different parts of the world, making friends with countless human beings of all races, religions, cultures, languages, genders, socioeconomic levels, ages, and every other distinction you can think of. These experiences in particular led me to the conclusion that love is the only power that transcends all differences, because these friendships have proven it.

bell hooks talks about love as a choice, arguing that we do not have to love, but instead we choose to do so. Friendship is the finest example of love as a choice, because it entails the conscious decision and active striving towards wholeheartedly embracing other human beings with the unwavering commitment to love them. We do not get to choose our families, but we do *choose* our friends; the connections we make go beyond gender, race, language, culture, or other superficialities. I continue to feel inspired when I witness how people from completely opposite corners of the world can meet and get to know each other, love each other, and become friends.

As I've gotten older I've realized that time is not the proper unit to measure the significance of a friendship. An increment of time cannot capture the depth, magnitude, and density of the profound connection that can happen between people when we become vulnerable and reveal our most inner being and time and space cease to separate us. Time does not do friendship justice. What are seconds, minutes, hours, days, months, and years next to this connection that allows me to *feel* and to *be* whole?

An unspoken covenant exists between friends, a certain knowledge that doesn't need to be proclaimed, an inherent trust that flourishes, where it's never necessary to say "don't tell anyone." Friendship thrives in authenticity. That's where its power lies: there is no pretense, no cover up, no faking. In your rawest possible self you are saying, "Here I am; this is me," and I am answering back, "I see you. I love you."

Friendship goes beyond *accepting* to *embracing* another person wholly. Friendship is like sand: imagine a sandcastle that you build together. You can spend all the time in the world building the structure, making it big or small, tall or short, intricate and ornate, or spare and minimalistic. You build together, even though you know it will be washed away by the sea. You continue, because even when it does get washed away, the sand still lingers, in a different form. Like friendship, sand takes on a particular shape in that moment in time; it's malleable and adjustable, and no matter what shapes and forms you build, and no matter how many times it dissolves again into the large expanse of the beach, it doesn't cease to exist. It's always there.

Friendships come in all shapes and sizes. I don't mean to suggest that longevity in friendships is irrelevant or unimportant--there is a special bond that exists when people share a history. Like a treasure hidden in the past, when old friends get together they open the chest and explore its belongings, some that only they can decipher and value together. How wonderful it is to share a past, to reminisce with old friends! But magic also occurs when new friends bond and savor that deep connection.

I have always felt like a bird, flying free, seeking, roaming, and exploring our world. Even in my youth I was like a bird, but I always had a strong and safe nest to return to, where I received unconditional love from my family. Having this nest allowed me to cultivate my self-love and my love for others. As I flew farther and farther away from home, that love was put to the test, and what happened was extraordinary: it grew.

Through the cultivation of friendships across the world, I came to the conclusions that we can *learn* how to love, and that love in action can change the world. This was the birth of Lovescaping.

In *Letters to a Young Poet,* Rainer Maria Rilke stated, "For one human being to love another is perhaps the most difficult task of all, the epitome, the ultimate test. It is that striving for which all other striving is merely preparation." Lovescaping is my humble attempt to tackle this ultimate test, in hopes that our world will become a more loving place. Who am I to even attempt this "most difficult task"? Simply put, I am a human being who loves and is loved, and I have been a witness of the great power of love--its ability to transform and change people, its ability to heal, nurture and revive. Love is so powerful that it has allowed me to reach the conclusion that it is indeed *the* panacea for all our world's problems. I do not take this affirmation lightly, and I am serious when I claim that love can save our world.

My childhood was filled with the greatest of all privileges: unconditional love. I grew up with two mothers: my biological mom, Mami, and my non-biological mom, Mamajose, our nanny who joined our family right after my first sister was born. Growing up with two mothers allowed me to understand the transcendent and infinite power of love. Not even blood ties stand in the way of love. If they did, how could I love both of my mothers with such intensity? Love does not have a limit; there is no set amount of love that one can give or receive, and this makes it the most unique experience and expression for humanity.

Mami's world became a stage upon which my sisters and I were the protagonists of her play. She dedicated herself to raising us, supporting us at every step of our educational journey, sitting down at our little wooden table where we did our homework every day. She was invested in all of our after-school activities, read us our favorite books aloud, and always reminded us of how much she loved us. Mamajose bathed, dressed, fed, pampered and played with each one of us with meticulous and loving care, and we lived in constant awareness of her adoration. My dad, Papi, would put us to bed every night and sit on our beds and sing us each a lullaby while stroking our foreheads and hair until we fell asleep.

I grew up in Maracay, a small city 120 km west of Venezuela's capital, Caracas. Maracay is known as the "Garden City" because of its lush greenery, hills and mountains, grass, trees, and flowers of every size and every color, all around the city. Our house was at the foot of a small mountain, and we could see other bigger mountains at a distance. Our own home exemplified the Garden City's rich assortment of greeneries: in our garden we had mango trees, an avocado tree, some lemon trees, a *mamón* (Spanish lime) tree, banana trees, a eucalyptus tree, a grapefruit tree, a *pumarosa* (watery rose apple) tree, *cayena* (hibiscus) vines, and numerous other herbs, flower, and tree varieties. Many animals hung out as well: giant iguanas roamed around on the grass and climbed trees, hummingbirds drank the nectar from the flowers, and venomous cascabel snakes slithered in the leafy shadows. Many of my fondest childhood memories are of playing in our garden with my sisters and our friends.

We had a doll house, a treehouse, swings, a slide, and a seesaw; and we spent endless summer days playing outside despite the hot, humid weather. Our home was always filled with friends. We played everything from hide-and-go-seek to cops and robbers, *la candelita,* kick ball, and games that Mamajose would make up. Mamajose was a magnet for children: they all loved her, and we all pleaded for her to keep playing with us even after hours spent playing the same game. We loved getting sprayed by the water hose and making water balloons during Carnaval or just when the weather was hot. Against my parents' orders, my best friend and I would climb up and hide on our home's green roof, where we could see the full sky and mountains around us and dream about the world beyond ours.

I am the middle child, sandwiched between my two precious sisters, Tuti and Sofía. Growing up, Tuti and I were *uña y mugre,* inseparable, since we were only a little over a year apart. Sofía is four years younger than I am, and she was a mischievous, clever and unruly child. Tuti was the most beautiful baby ever born, with blue eyes the color of the Caribbean Sea and skin like a peach. She was the perfect baby by all measures; always happy, she rarely cried. When she turned one, she got an extremely high fever that changed her forever. Her condition has never been diagnosed, but the fever left her with a severe motor problem and significant developmental delays. Tuti is completely innocent: she will always be like a child, pure, honest and with no malice. She is the personification of love, and sharing my life with her has been the greatest gift I have ever received.

Tuti taught me many of the values that I have carried with me throughout my life, the values that have allowed me to become a Lovescaper. Despite all her difficulties and struggles she managed to succeed, to rise above and beyond her condition, to embrace the joy of being alive and spread it. For Tuti every small act was a victory, and our family celebrated it unapologetically. When she learned to walk, when she learned to run without falling, when she learned to talk, when she learned to write and read, when she learned to eat by herself, dress by herself, when she graduated high school--all these were feats for Tuti. We never took them for granted, and we understood the resilience it took for her to accomplish them.

This was the birth of gratitude for me, appreciating every single detail and minute of my life, no matter how small it was. Tuti never complained, even with the suffering she endured through numerous medical tests, painful procedures, and experimental treatments to try to discover a cure for her condition. Watching Tuti, I learned to think twice before complaining; I have never taken for granted the most essential parts of my existence, like being healthy and having the ability to use all my faculties.

Growing up next to a child with special needs inevitably changes your perspective on life. I developed a sensibility that allowed me to appreciate and value all the different forms of existence on our planet. From early on, I learned that there are many nuances that make human beings unique and special. That there is not one right or wrong way, but many different ways. I learned the importance of diversity and integration, and I learned the fundamental lesson that everyone can teach us something. Always. No exceptions.

Tuti taught me the value of patience, of learning to wait while she got dressed, or ate, or drew. Tuti also embraced her role as big sister and became my fiercest protector when we were children. During our early years, I was a passive, fearful child who would remain paralyzed like a statue whenever somebody hurt me. Tuti would not take it; she would wham her lunchbox at the kids who bothered me, especially those who pulled my hair and made me cry. Never again would they dare mess with me. She taught me to stand up for myself, to lose my fear, and to spread my wings wide. Tuti taught me to be disciplined, to persevere, and to be courageous. As we got older, the courage she instilled in me made me become her fierce defender, as well as that of anybody who was excluded or marginalized in society.

Growing up with Tuti wasn't easy. I had to learn to cope with feelings of guilt, shame, and rejection. I went through a period of time where I was annoyed to be with my sister, where I felt like she held me back, and even felt ashamed to be with her. For most of my life however, the feeling I have struggled with the most has been guilt: guilt because I was "normal" and she wasn't; guilt because she couldn't do the things that I could; guilt because "Why her and not me?" It took many years to cross that bridge from guilt to empathy, but crossing that bridge made me understand my sister and her condition in a whole new light: Tuti was happy living her life, and she didn't for one second resent the fact that we were different.

Mami battled every day to integrate Tuti into our world. She taught our whole community that there is no shame in being different. I admire the determination with which she fought (and still fights!) to include Tuti in as many activities as possible. Mami worried that Sofía and I would resent her because she gave Tuti so much attention, that we would think she didn't love us as much as she loved our sister.

But our entire family crossed that bridge from guilt to empathy, and we learned that love does not become diminished when shared. Even when Mami or Papi weren't physically around, we always had an army of love surrounding us: Mamajose, my grandmother Atita, my uncles, and numerous other friends and family members. As a family, we went through ups and downs as every family does, but we never lost sight of the most important thing: love. I will never forget something Papi once told me: "Do you know where our home is?" he said. "It's where Tuti is."

Yes, love was fundamental to my childhood. But in the outside world, when I had to interact with people I'd never met before, people who were different from me, who didn't know my story, who had different beliefs, different value systems, different languages, different cultures, that love was put to the test.

I took my family's love that had nurtured me and carried it to the outside world.

There, Lovescaping became possible.

uBuntu and Friendship

I learned about uBuntu for the first time while living in Mozambique in 2010. uBuntu has its roots in the Bantu languages of southern Africa, and it means "I am because you are" or "I am because we are." uBuntu is not just a word, but a way of life, a philosophy, a way of knowing, a way of living together in community and living through each other, with one another. In uBuntu, there is no championing of individualism. On the contrary, there is no "I" without "you," no "I" without "we;" our existence is dependent on each other's. Like a giant spider web, we are all interconnected. uBuntu is lived daily through actions and through an incredible display of solidarity.

Think for a moment about one of the staple Western philosophical tenets put forth by Descartes: *cogito ergo sum,* "I think, therefore I am." What does *to be* mean? This question has puzzled human beings from the beginning of time. In Descartes' definition to be is to think. This is one way to define existence, but I think it's insufficient. Contrast this with uBuntu philosophy and realize that even if you think, you are not—in fact cannot *be*--without me. I am, not just because I think, but because you are. Under this paradigm, there is no conception of existence as solitary individuals who use their brains to think; but instead, there is a sense of solidarity, an interdependence between all humans. When I think about uBuntu, I think about friendships, how they form, how they come to fruition, and how we grow to rely on them for solace, support and hope.

To share Lovescaping with you, I have to start with Mozambique. Because it was there where I learned that contemplating death leads to love. There is no other way to begin understanding Lovescaping than with the story of Elias. It is a story of friendship, life, love and death. Death helps us remember the evaporative nature of life: like a fog, it can come and go, sometimes unexpectedly and suddenly. Death allows me to appreciate every single opportunity I have to breathe and to love everything around me. It also binds me to the rest of humanity.

> *No man is an island entire of itself; every man*
> *is a piece of the continent, a part of the main;*
> *if a clod be washed away by the sea, Europe*
> *is the less, as well as if a promontory were, as*
> *well as any manner of thy friends or of thine*
> *own were; any man's death diminishes me,*
> *because I am involved in mankind.*
> *And therefore never send to know for whom*
> *the bell tolls; it tolls for thee."*
>
> -   *John Donne (1624)*

Elias

I met Elias on a Tuesday afternoon in May 2010 when I attended a seminar for community volunteers on tuberculosis. Tuberculosis is the number one cause of death for people with HIV. In Mozambique, the number of tuberculosis victims is increasing each year, even though it is curable. Mr. Martins, a nurse with many years of experience at the hospital, was training local volunteers to inform communities on ways to prevent and treat tuberculosis. The seminar was held in the local language, Shangana, but all the pamphlets were in Portuguese. Mr. Martins would translate the most important points for me. Wearing an impeccable white uniform and glasses that magnified the size of his eyes, he had a large, flat nose and a round belly. He walked with his feet nearly spread out horizontally. An accomplished public speaker, he liked to quiz his participants to make sure that they had acquired the knowledge he so passionately delivered. We had a lunch break after the presentations were finished, and a few people who worked at the hospital came to join us.

Elias came for lunch. I noticed him immediately because he had a perfectly round face, observant black eyes, and a beautiful smile--his perfectly aligned teeth were the whitest I've ever seen. He was robust, with a potbelly. Sergio, the hospital's doctor, introduced me to him, "This is Elias, our lab technician," he said, and we shook hands. Elias had large hands, with thick fingers and hard palms. As he sat down to eat, his eyes moved quickly in all directions, surveying everything around him, like a lion who examines its prey before making a move. He ate hungrily. Ms. Esther, who was in charge of the food, remarked, "Elias eats with such gusto; I just love to watch him eat!" She cackled with laughter. After he finished eating, he left, and I couldn't help but notice in him an air of superiority.

That week I went three times to the hospital but didn't see Elias, because I stayed in the maternity section with the nurses. On Friday night I went to my friend

Mercedes' house for dinner. As I approached the house, I heard the sweet tune of a guitar and voices singing at the balcony. To my great surprise it was Elias playing the guitar.

"Hi! It's nice to see you again! Have you been going to the hospital?" he asked me as I sat down next to him to sing along.

"Yes, I have, but I haven't seen you!" I said. "I've been working in the maternity section."

"Why haven't you come to the lab? I need a lot of help there!" he said.

"I will come next week," I replied as Mercedes handed me a tonic water.

Elias played a melody, and we made up lyrics for it, in both English and Portuguese. Elias' English was very good, and he wanted to practice and improve. I told him I had evening lessons for the more advanced students and he could join. Thrilled, he said he would come on Monday.

We laughed, sang, and took pictures. From that night onwards, Elias and I would sit together and improvise songs. His ability to come up with endlessly different tunes and lyrics impressed me. On that first night he sang a sweet tune with a personalized chorus that went,

"On the plane,

Irene comes

To Mozambique,

Tonight...

Too-ru-ru-ru..."

I couldn't make out the exact lyrics of the rest of the song, but it mentioned a number of different animals that I would see in Mozambique, including zebras and lions. Every time he had the guitar with him I would ask him to play and sing it for me.

We finished our dinner and it was getting late. Elias offered to walk me home, so we left the house and crossed the street. We passed an empty bar that had three pool tables and Elias went in.

"Do you know how to play?" he asked me.

When I said no, he motioned to an old man who was sitting in the corner and gave him some money.

He began to play and showed me how to position the cue and my body, how to aim and how to choose which ball to hit. I tried, without success.

"Come on, you can do it! You need to hit the ball with confidence. Keep your eye on the ball, on your target--concentrate!" Elias helped me with the grip, and I managed to hit one ball successfully. I was happy.

"I knew you could do it! Easy, right?" and he smiled.

After that, we walked by small shops lined up one next to the other along the sandy road. A group of people gathered around one particular shop. A potpourri of Michael Jackson music was playing, and a thin man was dancing in the middle, moving to the beat better than Michael Jackson himself. He was incredibly flexible and swift, one of those gifted people who appears to be born for the sole purpose of moving their bodies. Elias and I were impressed. I couldn't resist joining the dancer, and so I stepped inside the circle. Everyone cheered, "*Mulungo* dancing, *mulungo* dancing!" I closed my eyes and let my body flow to the rhythm of the upbeat song.

Elias stood with the others in the circle, watching us dance and cheering. When the song finished and Elias and I said goodbye to the group, I asked for the man's name, the one who moved his body like a serpent. "Joaquim," one of the group replied, because the man kept dancing, completely absorbed in his music.

That night marked the beginning of a beautiful friendship between Elias and me. We became best friends and colleagues; I taught him English and he taught me everything that had to be learned at the lab. He taught me how to diagnose malaria by looking for plasmodium in the microscope. He taught me how to single out Koch's bacillus in the microscope to diagnose tuberculosis. He taught me how to determine a person's blood type and how to take blood samples. He gave me lessons about blood cells, HIV and numerous other diseases. We were a team, inseparable, indestructible. When we worked together at the lab we would finish our work in half the time.

Wednesdays were the busiest day at the lab, because, apart from the normal routine of hundreds of patients coming in to get tested for malaria and other maladies, we needed to take blood samples from around a hundred people with HIV for the CD4 count. The blood samples were taken early in the morning from the patients and sent to Xai-Xai, a town further north where they had the necessary equipment to perform the test. HIV-infected people deal with a continuous reduction of their CD4 cells, a part of the immune system. Depending on how low the CD4 count is, it can be determined when the patient has AIDS and when medication should be administered. The count also helps us check how effective the medication has been in patients who are already taking antiretrovirals.

When we arrived at 7 a.m. to set everything up for the "CD4 Marathon" as we called it, there were patients already waiting outside. Some had come from far away or had to go to work early and wanted to be among the first in. They would place their papers with their exam orders in a box we had set up outside the lab. I was in charge of recording everything, and Elias took out the blood samples. The first step was to find the CD4 notebook and write the date and number the patients, one through one hundred. Next, I would collect the papers from the boxes outside and number those. Then a nurse would bring in a box of a hundred empty blood test tubes.

I was in charge of keeping track of all the test tubes. We would call patient number one, and the person with that number written on the exam paper would come up to us. I would write the patient's name on the notebook next to "1" then I would write "1" with a permanent marker on the blood test tube and pass it to Elias who would then extract the blood from the patient. The tube would be placed in a box along with its exam order, with the number and patient's name. This was a life-and-death task, and I had to make sure to check and double check that all the information was accurate and that each number assigned to each patient was indeed the same number on the test tube. I had a huge responsibility and had to make sure no mistakes were made; the patients' lives depended on it. Elias was a master at extracting blood samples, but even he struggled with several patients. No matter where in the arm he pinched, often blood would not flow out. It was an arduous task. I could see drops of sweat rolling down his face when he struggled to find a vein that would give him blood.

"No blood," he would sigh. "These people have no blood left!"

Some of the hardest patients were children. It was harrowing to see babies being brought to the lab to check their CD4 count. These babies were born with HIV. They battled, kicked, and screamed, and it sometimes took four of us to hold them down while Elias attempted to take blood from their arms. This spot often failed, so he almost always ended up taking blood from the jugular vein in the neck. Watching these children suffer while blood was extracted from their frail little bodies shattered my heart. But what made my heart break even more was the knowledge that these babies were born into the world with a treatable but incurable virus. The mother or caretaker bringing them in would help us to hold the child still; sometimes their faces showed sorrow and pain, and other times, indifference.

When we were alone, Elias would call me Madame, which in Portuguese has a stress on the "da," and was sometimes used in Mozambique as an endearing and respectful title. In our English lessons he called me Teacher, and at the lab he called me by my first name. To me, he was always Elias. We opened up to each other and talked about our lives: our past, our present and our future dreams. With these glimpses into his past, I started building a complete image of Elias, the same way he built his image of me. Elias was sharp, quick, and witty, and he never let an opportunity escape him. Once when we were walking back to my house from the lab, he told me a story about the time he was a teenager and worked at a perfume shop in Maputo, the capital of Mozambique.

"The owners were Indian. At the beginning they were terribly impolite and treated me with disdain. In their eyes I was always the 'Negro,' but despite that, they hired me and kept me for a while. Weeks went by, and the owner saw that I was a good salesman. Our sales went up dramatically, and the shop was making good money. He started treating me with more respect, and as time went by, the old Indian man grew fonder and fonder of me. So fond he grew, he started calling me 'son' and invited me to his family gatherings, and I became part of their family. I have to admit that I was a good salesman. In order to make more money, I would sell the perfumes at a higher price than they were marked and keep the difference for me." He interrupted our brisk walk and stopped to look at the expression on my face.

"I can see you doing that, Elias!" I laughed.

"Don't think wrong. I have never and will never steal! I was just making extra money for me, and it didn't harm anyone. The owners still made good money, and they were happy. So was I," he said.

"I never thought you were stealing, I was just thinking how clever you are," and I elbowed him on the arm.

He laughed, and I saw a smile of nostalgia for those long-gone times cross his lips.

"I had to leave the shop because I was studying, and the old Indian man was devastated. He grew older and older, and a few months later I found out he had died. I felt very sad and visited his family to offer my condolences. They were all extremely kind and seemed genuinely happy to see me. That was the last time I saw them. I don't even know if they still keep the shop," he concluded.

"Perhaps when you go to Maputo again, you can pass by and see if the shop is still there," I suggested.

"Nah! It would be too sad to walk by and discover that the shop doesn't exist anymore, I would rather not know," he said.

We walked on in silence under the still, starry sky, two wanderers lost in the past.

During my English lessons I always played music while the students did their exercises. One day, Elias asked me to compile a playlist and burn him a CD with guitar songs; he had an excellent ear and would pick up any tune, any note, after hearing it once. So I put together a number of different songs that featured the guitar as the main instrument. I gave him the CD, and he dutifully listened to all the songs. The next day he came back with his verdict: "The best one is the one with no lyrics, the classical guitar song. I want more of those!"

He was referring to a song played by Julian Bream. A while back, my dad had given me Julian Bream's "Ultimate Guitar Collection" CD, with a compilation of

Spanish classical guitar songs. I listened to it religiously.

"It's also my favorite," I said laughing. Unfortunately, I was never able to make him another CD because my laptop's CD drive crashed after burning CDs for everyone. However, I played Julian Bream's beautiful music during our lessons, and I could see Elias savoring every note while he completed his exercises.

One early evening, when Elias and I were about to leave the lab, a man walked in wanting to donate blood for a sick relative. He was awfully thin and had the saddest-looking eyes I had ever seen in my life. I felt sorry for him. He had been a blood donor in the past and brought with him a half-destroyed booklet that said his last donation took place in 2003. We followed the usual procedure for blood donors: we took a blood sample and tested him for HIV, Hepatitis B, syphilis, and malaria. Elias and I waited next to the counter where the four rapid tests were reacting with the chemicals and the blood of the patient to see if they were negative or positive. The man stood outside while we waited for the results. Most of the time, when the results from the rapid tests were positive, they showed up within the first couple minutes. I looked down and to my utter surprise, all four tests were positive, *all four of them*! I could not believe it. This poor man walked in the lab not even knowing that he had malaria, let alone HIV, wanting to donate blood. It was devastating. I looked at Elias helplessly and he nodded--he had evidently encountered this situation numerous times. I was "used to" people having HIV and malaria by now, but this particular situation was new for me. I was shocked. Elias discarded all the tests in the rubbish bin, sighed and said, "Well, Madame, that's life."

"What will you tell him?"

"I will tell him that he can't donate blood, and that he should come back tomorrow morning if he wants to know the results and get treatment," Elias said while he took off his white robe.

"Elias, that man is dying, and he doesn't have a clue," I said with a shaky voice.

"We are all dying, Madame," and he stepped outside the lab to talk to the man.

Patients reserved the right to know if they had HIV or not, and a vast majority preferred not to know. Elias was a pro, and he knew how to talk to patients, how to let them know, in a subtle way, that they were ill. Shortly after that incident, we had a similar one that left my heart feeling like a wounded soldier in the middle of the battlefield. We were about to close when a short, thin man came panting inside the lab.

"My name is Rogerio Rodrigues, I need to donate blood for my sick wife who is dying from severe anemia," he said running out of breath.

Elias asked him to sit down and take a deep breath.

"Calm down brother. Have you ever donated blood before?" Elias asked him.

"Only once, a long time ago. I must save me wife; she's all I have in the world," he said on the verge of tears.

He handed us his identification card and a piece of paper from the in-patient department that said his wife needed type A blood.

"Our blood type is compatible," he added and buried his decrepit face in his hands. Rogerio Rodrigues was thirty-two years old, but looked sixty. He was so thin that I didn't see how he could donate 500ml of blood. I sat next to him and put my hand on his back.

"Brother, we need to perform some tests before you can donate blood," Elias said.

"Yes, yes, do whatever you have to do," he said in his crumbling voice.

Elias took a blood sample and asked him to wait outside while we performed the tests. After what had happened with the sad-faced man, I was somewhat prepared for similar results. Rogerio looked everything but healthy and strong.

"He looks so sick, how is he ever going to be able to donate blood for his wife?" I asked Elias.

"I don't know. But look at this! His hemoglobin is fine, at 15-16, I'm surprised. Let's see what the other results tell us." We performed the usual: HIV, syphilis, malaria, and Hepatitis. We waited in silence. Five minutes later the results were negative. Ten minutes later the results were still negative.

"We need to wait fifteen minutes at least," Elias said.

Fifteen minutes later and still all the results were negative. Elias and I looked at each other in disbelief.

"Well, he's healthy. Let's confirm his blood type then," Elias said. We took out the strips and the solutions we used to determine blood type and Rogerio was type A as he had told us. Elias called him back in the lab.

"Ok, brother, let's try this," Elias told him. A hint of hope glowed in Rogerio's sunken face. He lay on the stretcher and rolled his long sleeve shirt up to expose his bony arm. He started talking while Elias searched for the right vein.

"My wife is twenty-three years old. I have suffered so much in my life, but ever since I met her, my life changed. I learned what happiness and love are about. She is everything I've got--I don't know what to do without her. She is so weak. I can't eat, I can't sleep, I can't think. I have to save her life. She is all I've got; her disease has consumed me entirely," Rogerio spoke quickly, hardly ever pausing, and his glassy eyes stared into mine pleading for help. My eyes were watery, but to give Rogerio strength and hope I refrained from letting the tears escape.

"You have to press this yellow ball," Elias instructed him after he had found a vein. Rogerio just needed to pump blood into the bag.

Rogerio pressed that yellow ball like his life depended on it, but only a small amount of blood came out, like a faint stream about to disappear from the land. It was dry.

Elias tried different veins and switched arms but still, only a small amount of blood flowed out. Rogerio kept pressing the ball and saying, "I must save my wife; she's all I've got." Tears flowed out from his glassy eyes. "I've been looking everywhere for people to donate blood, but I can't find anyone!"

"Rogerio, I would gladly donate for your wife, but my group is not compatible, I'm so sorry. We'll keep looking. We'll find someone--don't lose hope!" I said.

Rogerio's love for his wife was illuminating. I was moved to tears for that love. If his wife died, he would die with her too. His existence depended on their love, and without her, life had no meaning. Defeated, Rogerio stood up and shook my hand and Elias'.

"Thank you for your kindness. Now I will try to find someone to donate blood for my wife. I won't rest until I find someone," he said resolutely.

"Rogerio, you will find someone, we will also try our best to find blood for your wife. We're here to help you, don't forget," I said.

"Brother, you will save your wife. Be strong and never lose hope," Elias said.

"Thank you, thank you so much," he said as he left the lab.

If sadness had a face, it would have Rogerio's.

Elias and I sat next to each other for a few long minutes, thinking about Rogerio and his wife, and their love.

"He really loves her, doesn't he?" I said to Elias.

"That man is so in love with her that he would die for her," Elias replied.

"Would you ever give your life for someone?" I asked him.

"Of course, Madame. I would give my life without hesitation for the people I love. Would you?"

"Of course... for the people I love in the world," I replied.

Just then I felt an irresistible urge to cry, and like a dam opening its floodgates, tears gushed out of my eyes.

"What's the matter, Madame? Why are you crying?" Elias asked, frightened.

I couldn't speak. As I succumbed entirely to the intense feeling of sadness, Elias realized there was nothing he could say to soothe my crying. He just put his arm around my shoulders and sat next to me as I cried and shook uncontrollably for fifteen minutes. As I started calming down, Elias dared to speak again,

"Why are you crying so hard?"

"Oh Elias! Life is so unfair, so cruel!" I said between sobs.

"Madame, life is just the way it is. Don't beat yourself for the things you see here at the hospital. Life is sad but also happy, cruel but also beautiful," he said.

"Thank you Elias. I'm sorry you had to witness this, I feel better now after crying. Thank you for holding me. With you I feel safe; I feel like everything is going to be alright," I answered.

"You don't have to thank me, and you don't have to say sorry, Madame. Please! You know how much I care for you, and I'm always here to hug you and listen to you whenever you feel sad. But I don't like seeing you like this! Come on, give me a smile," he pleaded. I smiled, and he gave me a pat in the back.

"That's more like the Madame I know!" he said, winking at me.

"Wash your face and take off your robe. It's late, and we have to go home," he said.

We put everything away, turned off the lights, locked the doors, and stepped into a cold and windy night.

The wind roared ferociously, and the trees shook violently along the way. Elias gave me his windbreaker.

"What about you?" I asked him.

He laughed. "Madame, don't you worry about me, I'm double your size--you need it more than I do."

We walked side-by-side, sticking to each other, advancing against the unwavering wind. We arrived at my place and sat on the stairs that led up to my room for a few minutes. It was cold and the palm trees in the patio danced incessantly with the wind.

"Do you feel better, Madame?" Elias asked. "I'm worried about you."

"Yes, I feel better. Thanks to you Elias."

"I don't want you to be scared. Nothing bad will ever happen to you as long as I'm here. Don't you worry Madame. I will always protect you," he said.

"Thank you, Elias. I know you will. And I will always do my best to protect you, too. You know that, right?" I asked him.

"Sure," he said, and he started laughing.

"Why are you laughing?" I asked him.

"Because I just imagined you protecting me against a great big bully, bigger than you, even bigger than me..." and we both burst into laughter.

"Ok, Elias, go home. It's late, cold, and windy. We had a long day at the lab today," I said.

"Are you sure you're alright? I can stay longer with you if you'd like."

I smiled. "You already made me laugh! I feel much better already. Thank you!"

"No need to thank me, remember? And just call me if you start feeling sad again--do you promise?"

"I promise." We stood up and hugged.

"Until tomorrow..."

Elias was in charge of finding blood donors and keeping the hospital's blood bank, which consisted of a small refrigerator at our lab. This was one of the most challenging jobs at the hospital, because the rate of HIV was so high and the people were afraid to get tested and discover the truth. We hardly ever had blood in our refrigerator, but blood was always needed for malaria patients with severe anemia. Once I donated blood for a little girl who was dying from anemia. Elias was much opposed to having me donate, but I insisted to the point that he gave in. I donated as much as I could before I fainted. Elias carried me in his arms repeating, over and over, "You're never doing this again."

The severe shortages of blood pained me to the heart. We always needed far more than we had. Elias had done a course and was an expert on the subject. In our lab, there was a whiteboard with important information posted along with a paper I had hand-written about the tests performed at the lab. On the left-hand border, Elias had proudly lined up photos from all the blood donors he had found. He could point to one of them and tell me the person's life story.

It was rumored that there was a "blood business" going around, and blood came at a high price. I heard countless stories from the nurses at our hospital that it was not uncommon for hospitals in Mozambique to exchange blood for money, something that was illegal. Blood was supposed to be available at the hospitals for transfusions at no cost whatsoever. I never saw any sort of illegal transaction going on in our hospital, and Elias was truly passionate about finding donors and handling the blood according to protocol. We worked on several blood donation campaigns; and, through them, we managed to collect a few good samples.

The blood donation campaigns operated under a "zero discrimination policy," which meant anyone who was willing to donate blood, would get a quick check for hemoglobin level, blood pressure, weight, and what

Elias called "general appearance." If they passed these tests, we would collect the blood. Only back at the lab would we check for HIV and other maladies. It was so disheartening going back to the lab to check the blood samples and discover so many were unusable: we had to throw them away. We used incentives to get donors, such as providing a sandwich and juice after the blood was collected; and if the patients became regular blood donors, they had priority access at the hospital. So many of these patients who volunteered to donate would tell us, "If my blood is not good, please don't tell me."

Once, we went to the Universal Church of the Kingdom of God to collect some blood. Dr. Claudia, the hospital's chief and only doctor, Elias and I met early on Sunday morning at the lab to collect the necessary equipment to carry to the church in the hospital's ambulance. Elias gave me one of his shirts: a yellow t-shirt that says, "*Dou o melhor de mim para salvar vidas: Dou sangue*," (I give my best to save lives: I give blood).

To this day, I carry that yellow shirt with me everywhere I go.

We were excited about this opportunity. Elias had spoken to the pastor, and he had been very supportive of our cause and said we could set up on Sunday morning after the service. We arrived at the church before the service ended and sat at the back. It was the first time I had ever entered a Universal Church. The church was a large building, white and barren, with rows of benches where the followers sat and an altar space at the back of the church where a cross hung on the wall and a pastor walked incessantly back and forth and spoke in an extremely loud voice over a microphone. The church was packed, and the people were performing exorcisms as we sat down. At the altar, a woman had her eyes closed. She moved her head in circles as the pastor placed his hand on her head and exclaimed: *"SAI DEMONIO, SAI!" (LEAVE, DEMON, LEAVE!)*.

Everyone in the church echoed these words over and over again, as if they were casting a spell. The pastor repeated the words on the microphone, magnifying the sound and blasting it through the benches, out the windows, out the door, resonating in our ears. He raised his arms up in the air and the congregation echoed his movements.

Elias, Dr. Claudia and I looked at each other in disbelief. We were the only ones inside the church who were not yelling and raising our arms. Five hosts walked the main aisle--young men and women wearing a white sash around their bodies. I recognized one of the girls; she was a teacher at the nuns' preschool right behind our house. Their job was to carry people to the altar or assist anyone who needed help during the ceremony. As the voices intensified and the possessed woman at the altar appeared almost paralyzed, the pastor signaled the congregation to stop. Apparently, the demons had left the woman, and she was cured. She was carried off the altar by two of the host boys. We sat in awe. I whispered to Elias, "This is scary." He nodded.

Music followed, blasting again on the microphone. Everyone sang along. The pastor was a man in his forties, short and somewhat chubby. He talked incessantly, even with the music, but the sounds were so loud I couldn't make out a word of what he was saying. After the music stopped it was time for the people to give out money. The word "*aliança*" was mentioned at least hundred times, and later I understood he was referring to some rings. A few people went up to the altar and lined up.

As the pastor called them, they approached him and put some money in a bowl. The pastor raved about the amount given. Those who gave more money received a ring, the "*aliança,*" and more praise from the pastor. I looked around me and saw the people struggling to give out whatever they could, and their weary looks suggested that this money was their weekly or even monthly wage. And they were giving it all up for the sake of the "*aliança*" and God's help. Whenever someone dropped money in the bowl, the pastor assured that person, "You are helping Jesus and Jesus will help you!"

When you give money to the pastor, Jesus will help you? I wondered.

The pastor immensely praised those people who gave 100 and even 200 meticals. His voice roared and thundered through the speakers: *Amen! Amen! Amen!* After the aliança process ended, the pastor announced our mission.

"Today we welcome our guests from the hospital who have come here with an important mission: that of collecting blood. I hope all of you do the very Christian duty of donating blood. I encourage each one of you to donate blood today to save the lives of our dear brothers and sisters. I will be the first one to do so and set the Christian example!"

He was neither the first nor the last: he never donated blood.

He continued, "I welcome our doctor to come up here and talk to our congregation about the importance of giving blood. Amen!"

Everyone clapped as Dr. Claudia went up to the altar. When the pastor first mentioned that we were there to collect blood, I heard frightened gasps around the public. Dr. Claudia explained the procedure and her hopes that we would collect as much blood as possible to fill our empty blood bank. Her petite figure and soft voice stood in stark contrast to the pastor. Elias motioned to me to begin setting up our equipment: stretchers, syringes, bags, alcohol, squeezable balls, tape, markers, patient-cards and food. We began to set up as the pastor finished the service, and Dr. Claudia joined us.

The mass of people began moving towards the exit where we were positioned, many of them trying to sneak out. A few brave ones approached us, and I filled their information cards and wrote their names on the blood bags as Dr. Claudia checked for Hemoglobin, blood pressure, and weight. Elias was ready waiting by the stretchers to find the right vein. We managed to obtain eight donors; the others were frightened to death and would not even approach us. The entire time, the pastor was nowhere to be seen, but we were still hopeful that he would appear to fulfill his public statement of being the first to perform his Christian duty.

When there was nobody else left and we had started to clean up, the pastor popped up as if by magic and patted Elias on the back.

"You got a few bags there. I'm glad."

"Pastor, aren't you going to donate?" Elias asked him.

"No, son, not today. Maybe some other time." And he extended his hand out to Dr. Claudia and I for a handshake. I was very upset. He had lied. Not just to us, but to an entire congregation who faithfully believed every word he said and followed his example.

"Thank you for allowing us to come here today," said Dr. Claudia. I was too upset to thank him or to pretend, so I resolved to keep quiet. Elias glanced at me with his quick-moving eyes and gave me a look that said, "*I know exactly how you feel.*"

"Well, that was quite an experience," said Dr. Claudia as we waited outside the church for the ambulance to take us back.

"Now we have to check the blood at the lab. Let's hope most of them are good," Elias said.

The three of us discussed the service and Elias described what we had witnessed. "Those people are hypnotized; that is the work of magic. They do anything the pastor tells them to do. They give him all their money, and they don't realize he's rich."

"What bothered me the most was his unscrupulousness!" I said, so disappointed. "He lied with such nerve!"

"This is the way things work in these places. Let's look on the bright side--at least we didn't leave empty-handed," Elias said, putting his hand on my shoulder. The three of us jumped in the ambulance and left the Universal Church of the Kingdom of God behind in a whirlwind of sand and dust. I looked out the window one last time, hoping that the people would truly be saved.

***

During our shift at the lab, Elias always made sure we took a break to eat. Sometimes he brought food from home, sometimes we bought bread and *bagia*, nuggets made with a particular type of bean, at the hospital's tiny canteen, and sometimes we ate leftovers from the hospital's kitchen. We usually sat under a huge mango tree by the hospital's kitchen and ate the food with our hands. Those breaks were very important to us. Under the mango tree, we were away from illness and death, and for a moment forgot the ravaging conditions just a few meters away. We laughed, joked, discussed, fought, and ate. Elias always made me eat more, and he was proud of himself when I gained weight.

"Remember when you arrived, Madame? You were so thin! And now you are strong and healthy," he said.

"You mean I'm fat, don't you?" I said laughing.

"Not fat, strong!" he said. "It's a good thing!" We both laughed.

One day, after a particularly tough morning, we were both exhausted. We collapsed on the roots of the mango tree and leaned against its old, rugged trunk.

"Elias, is it ever unbearable for you to confront so much death?" I asked him.

"At the beginning it's always difficult. But you get used to it, and you learn that death is just another part of life. It's my job to find the cause of someone's ailment in hopes that they will be cured or at least get treatment."

"You are so good at your job, so talented. I'm really proud of you," I told him. He turned his head towards me, surprised at my sudden comment.

"Thank you. Do you know what I think, Madame? I think you should study to be a lab technician. You learn very quickly, and we work so well together. You could do it in no time!" he said persuasively, moving his eyes from the branches up high back to me.

"Well, at one point I did consider studying medicine, but I wasn't ever completely convinced. And I do love working with you, and I know how much value your job has here; we need more people like you! But I don't think I'm going to be a lab technician," I told him. "I want to do something else, something that will enable more people to become lab technicians like you and have opportunities to improve their lives!" Elias didn't reply immediately but thought on my words.

"Madame, you are truly something else. We need you here. You need to stay and help us!"

"Elias, I'm leaving in September. But you know I'll come back!" I said.

"Why are you leaving in September?"

"My visa expires and I need to go back and continue my journey. I want to get a Master's degree; I need to work on my project from outside and find more help and more people to support us here in Mozambique. Of course I'll come back. You know I love this place, and I love you all. I don't want to leave, but I know that I have to. I will come back, don't worry." I said reassuringly.

"You can't leave us," Elias said with a sigh.

We sat in silence and ate our food. In the distance, we saw a group of barefoot boys running and singing happily. Elias broke the silence.

"I've always thought that we made a mistake by inventing shoes. Humans should roam the land barefoot to stay connected to the earth, just like monkeys. Our shoes isolate our bodies from the earth's energy, and if we had that connection, we would reduce illnesses, because we would stay connected to our earth."

"I agree with you. When I am barefoot and I feel my feet touching the moist, rich earth I do feel a difference, a special bond to the earth." I said.

"Yes, Madame, that's what I'm talking about."

Under that mango tree we also had our first real argument. It happened after Elias had become a regular in my English lessons. We were eating a salad with bread when Elias brought up the subject.

"I talked to the Administrator of the hospital, and she told me she was interested in your English lessons."

"Oh great! Did you tell her where we have our lessons and the schedule? She can join our classes any time!" I said, munching on lettuce.

"Actually, she doesn't like the idea of joining the group," Elias said tentatively. "She wants you to give her private lessons in her house."

"My lessons are open to everyone in Macia, there is no exclusivity, and I have plenty of different slots when she can come to the Missionary House and receive her lessons." I said.

"But since she is the Administrator, she thought that you--"

"I don't care if she's the President of the Republic. Everyone is welcome at my lessons in the Missionary House. I don't give preferential treatment to anyone. I'm indifferent whether it's the beggar on the street coming for lessons or the Administrator of this hospital. If she wants to learn, she can come to the lessons at the Missionary House. I'm not going to make a special time to teach her individually in her house."

"But--"

"No but, Elias. You should know this about me by now. I don't give preferential treatment!" I replied determinedly.

"I understand. And I know what you mean, but even in a poor country like Mozambique, there is a hierarchy. She will never come to our lessons and mix with us," he said.

"Well, that's her own problem. It's too bad she won't mix with us. That's her loss!" I answered and shrugged my shoulders. I noticed Elias was studying my face and thinking about my reasoning. In a way I think it struck him as odd.

Elias shrugged his shoulders too and kept eating.

"Tell her that my answer is that I would be delighted if she joined our lessons at the Missionary House." And with that, the discussion ended.

A few days later, out of the blue, Elias said, "You were right about what you said regarding the Administrator. I agree with you. We are all equal."

I smiled. A victory had been won.

Elias always understood and supported me. We both admired each other, and I think that made our relationship so special. Another day, under the big mango tree, when a breeze cooled our sweaty and sticky bodies, he said, "I know what you want."

"What do you mean?" I asked perplexed.

"I mean, what you want from a relationship," he said, clearing his throat.

"And what would that be, according to you?"

"Safety, protection. You want to feel safe. That is what you want," he declared triumphantly.

"How did you come up with that? Why do you think that?" I asked him.

"I just know it. I know you, and I know that's what you need." Elias was extremely observant, and he didn't miss a single detail, a single word, a single gesture.

"I don't know if that's true Elias. I think what I want most is to feel free. I love my freedom." I said.

"You need to feel safe."

"Well, don't we all like to feel safe? It is great to feel safe in the presence of someone you love, but I don't think that's the most important thing I want or need," I said.

"Trust me: it is safety. That's what you want," he said with such entitlement and certainty that I had nothing more to add. Just as mysteriously as that comment came up, it was dropped, and I never knew why Elias thought that or brought it up. If he only knew then how much thought I would put into that comment years later.

***

The Sunday I woke up with malaria symptoms I called Elias immediately.

"Elias, I have a pounding headache and a bitter taste in my mouth. I think I have malaria," I said over the phone.

"Ok, Madame, I'm coming for you. Let's get to the lab," he answered without hesitation.

Within twenty minutes, he was at the house. He surveyed me and declared, "Yes, I think you have malaria."

"How can you tell?" I asked him, surprised.

"Trust me: I can tell," he replied winking at me.

I felt exhausted, and just the walk to the hospital felt like a feat. The lab was closed on Saturdays and Sundays, and only when an emergency situation rose did the hospital staff contact Elias. It was early on Sunday morning, and most people were attending

Mass. When we arrived, Elias opened the lab with his key, and I plunged into a chair.

"Ok, let's run a rapid test and check in the microscope as well," he said. He pinched my finger and obtained a generous amount of blood. We put a drop inside the rapid test's small hole and added solution; the other sample was for the microscope. Blood for microscopic samples was placed on a slide that was then put to dry on a special machine that looked like a grill, then immersed in special ink and put to dry once more. Only then were they ready to be surveyed in the microscope. I sat waiting for the rapid test result, although already five minutes had gone by and only one line appeared on the result part. Elias was waiting for the microscope sample to dry.

"Once, my little girl fell very ill. She presented malaria symptoms, but we ran the malaria tests and they all came out negative. I knew she had malaria, but couldn't find the plasmodium in the microscope. I read and re-read my malaria books and came to the conclusion that she had a different type of malaria, not *falciparum*. Even though more than 90% of malaria cases here are *falciparum,* there was a chance that she had a different type. I spent entire nights searching until finally I found it; it was plasmodium *ovale,* I caught the little bastards in the microscope and was able to save my little daughter's life," Elias pronounced proudly.

"Wow, that is amazing... you mean these rapid tests only find *falciparum?*"

"Yes, because really, it's very rare to find a different type of malaria here. But my daughter, somehow, had *ovale.* Let me show you," he said as he opened his drawers and brought out a book. Elias always explained everything, showing me drawings and illustrations from his books. He opened a book to a page that explained the different types of malaria along with their respective illustrations of how the plasmodium shows up in the microscope. There are four different types of malaria: *falciparum, vivax, ovale* and *malariae.* The deadliest and most dangerous form is *falciparum,* which is the one that prevails in Mozambique and the whole of Sub-Saharan Africa.

"Do you notice that they all take on a different shape?" he asked me as he moved his index finger from one malaria type to the next.

"I can see they have different shapes, but I imagine it must be very difficult to distinguish them in the microscope," I said.

"Sometimes, you can spot the plasmodium right away, especially when they have spread and you see a bunch of them in a single microscopic field. But other times, they are hiding--or just beginning to spread, and it's hard to catch them," Elias explained. He stood up and submerged my dried blood sample in ink and placed it on the grill again. He came back and sat down next to me. Elias loved explaining biology to me. He was a talented teacher, and every time he explained something, I always understood.

"When was the last time you had malaria?" I asked him.

"A very long time ago, when I was a kid. I think I'm immune to it; as an adult I've never had it! Don't you see I'm a strong man?" he asked me laughing.

"Yes, I can see you're a strong man, but still, you must be careful. Malaria is not to be taken lightly. You know that better than anyone, I'm sure," I said.

"Madame, don't worry about me. Now let's worry about you. I'm a strong, black man. You are a fragile, white woman. You are at more risk than I am," he said.

"I'm not fragile!" I snapped.

"What I mean is, you are more *vulnerable* than any of us. We grew up with malaria and have developed some sort of immunity that obviously you don't have!

That is what I meant by fragile," he laughed. I laughed with him and he stood up to get the dried sample from the grill.

"The moment of truth," he said as he sat on the stool he used to look in the microscope.

I stayed in my chair, watching Elias' broad back as he stooped his head down to look in the microscope. A chilling silence followed for the next five minutes.

"Did you find anything?" I asked interrupting the silence.

"Not yet," he replied without moving from his position.

Silence followed for ten more minutes, and they felt longer than usual ones because I was keeping track of every second on the clock we had at the lab.

Elias hunted meticulously for the plasmodium until he finally gasped, "*Aha!*" and announced he had found something. I remember his words clearly: "How dare that bastard mosquito bite you, *mulungo*?"

"So I have malaria?" I asked impatiently.

"Yes, you do. Come here and see for yourself!" he added.

I stood up and went to the microscope. He stood up from his stool and gave me the seat.

"You have to look very carefully, do you see that small reddish mark that looks like a tiny bean?"

I focused the microscope and saw a bunch of blood cells but couldn't see the plasmodium. "I don't see it, Elias!"

I had seen the plasmodium numerous times before, but couldn't see it this time.

"You have plasmodium *falciparum*, one cross," he informed me as he wrote down on a sheet of paper the diagnosis: pf+.

When the malaria diagnosis was given, it came attached to crosses, which ranged from one to five. Contrary to popular belief, the number of crosses had nothing to do with the severity of the malaria. As I understood it, the number of crosses had to do with the amount of plasmodia that was found in a single microscopic field. One cross malaria meant that there was only one plasmodium in a single microscopic field. Five crosses malaria meant that there were over one hundred plasmodia in a single microscopic field. One cross malaria was said to be the most dangerous because it was the most resistant and it often had relapses.

"Don't worry, Madame. We'll get your medicine right away, and you'll be cured!" Elias said optimistically.

"Thanks for coming here on a Sunday with me Elias. I didn't want to wait until tomorrow," I said.

"Madame, I've already told you a million times. As long as I'm here, nothing bad will ever happen to you; and if there is anything I can do to help you, I will do it!"

"Thank you," I said approaching him and giving him a hug.

We left the lab and walked to the hospital's pharmacy to get the malaria medicine called Coartem, a combination of two drugs: artemether and lumefantrine. The treatment lasted three days and consisted of six doses. Luckily, I had the lightest malaria one could ever hope for. During those three days I stayed at home and recovered promptly.

I realized that Elias scrutinized me the same way he scrutinized a malaria sample. Years of practice and expertise at the lab had made him a master of observation. He placed me under the microscope and through the meticulous lens of observation, listening, and dialogue, searched deep inside my soul and discovered my weaknesses, insecurities, and fears, but also my strengths, dreams, and happiness. That is why he knew me so well and why our friendship had the depth it had. We understood and accepted each other entirely. Words were often superfluous for us; we were able to look each other in the eye and know exactly what the other was thinking. Aristotle's words "a friend is a single soul dwelling in two bodies," rang so true.

***

A couple of weeks before my departure, my oldest group of students announced they had a surprise for me. It was on a Friday night and they gave me instructions to wait inside our classroom. I had no idea what they were planning but I knew one thing for sure, Elias was leading the event.

On the appointed night I waited inside our classroom for my students to arrive. For some reason, I pictured them all coming to the classroom singing and dancing or something of the sort. But the night outside was quiet and there were no voices to be heard. I waited for ten minutes, then twenty minutes, and then decided to call Elias up.

I heard rattling and many voices in the background,

"Teacher, wait. Someone is coming to pick you up," he said hurriedly and hung up.

Five minutes later, my oldest student, Mr. Macie, poked his head inside the empty classroom and said with a smile, "Let's go, Teacher."

I followed him, asking, "Where are we going?"

"It's a surprise, Teacher!"

We walked under the starry sky, under the black canvas of silence, interrupted only by a few bars and houses where lights twinkled and merry Mozambican music played on the stereos. We took the road that led to Bilene and walked uphill and then downhill. We turned right into a neighborhood and followed the sounds of happy voices in the distance. We arrived at a house where I saw my students busy preparing huge pots of rice and chicken.

"Good evening, Teacher! You just wait right there. This is not all!" said Doles.

They were all working together to finish the feast. Elias walked out of the house.

"Welcome to my house!" he beamed.

Elias' house was blue. At the entrance there was a wide, inviting porch where all the students were busy moving pots and playing guitars. I stepped inside the house and saw a kitchen at the back and a spacious living room area at the entrance. Maria, Elias' shy and quiet sister-in-law, came out bursting with joy and hugged me.

"Welcome, Mana Irene!" she exclaimed.

"Where are your wife and baby girl?" I asked Elias.

"My wife is at school, and my little girl is sleeping," he said drying the sweat from his forehead.

Elias' wife was in her early twenties, but she hadn't finished high school. Elias enrolled her in evening lessons, so that she could finish her studies and get a job in the future. When he told me this the first time, I commended him for doing so, for recognizing the importance of education also for women, in this patriarchal society. He looked at me puzzled and replied, "But of course it's important for everyone! I told my wife when we married, 'you have to finish your studies!' Education is everything, Madame."

"This is a really nice house, Elias. I like it!" I said.

"Yes, the hospital provided it. It's comfortable, and the right size for us," he said smiling. There was music playing on the stereo, and all my students looked ecstatic.

"Everything is ready!" yelled Lizete as she closed one of the pots and motioned for everyone to get ready.

"Are we going somewhere else?" I asked.

"Yes, Teacher, follow us!"

In a procession, I followed my students out the house, back onto the main road. Each one of them was carrying something--giant pots, plates, cups, cutlery, bottles, chairs, tables, a guitar, and basins. We filled the still night with laughter and chatter, and in the darkness I could make out the outlines of my students carrying loads on their heads.

We arrived at our destination, a small bar on the road to Bilene. It consisted of a squared space, with red rails at the entrance and along one of the sides, and a bar at the back. It was a small space, but fresh and filled with joy. The students diligently set the tables in the middle, covered them with a white tablecloth, and placed everything else they had brought with them on the tables. They asked me to sit down while they all gathered around the table standing and started singing in Shangana, clapping their hands and snapping their fingers. When they finished the song, they all stood on the other side of the table, facing me.

Elias took out a piece of paper and spoke. "Dear Teacher, we wrote these words for you in both English and in Portuguese. We hope the English translation is correct," and they all laughed.

He read out the letter in English first,

Message from students to our friend and teacher Irene, because of her saying goodbye, after long time of staying and good living with others.

Your students feel well to be with you because the wise way that Teacher Irene has given us during her staying in this beautiful country, "Mozambique."

You leave us with longing, and graceful and we know that you also take with you our longing and graceful. We wish you a good travel, God bless you and find your family that for long time has been waiting, that is why we send our huge greetings for all your friends and relatives.

Good luck, until a day.

Many emotions were bubbling up inside me like an over-poured champagne glass, I was so moved, on the verge of tears. I experienced an immense feeling of joy and love in my heart, a feeling that made my body feel warm and my smile wide and permanent. My eyes twinkled with gratitude.

"Now I will read the Portuguese version of the letter in case certain things didn't make sense in the English translation," he said laughing. He read out the letter in Portuguese and the English translation remained true to the original one.

"Longing and graceful" was the translation they used for my favorite word in Portuguese, *"saudades."*

Saudades means missing someone or something, but it has more depth and feeling than the English expression, 'I miss you.' So the word 'longing' is quite appropriate. In Portuguese, you can use the word on its own--you can just tell or write someone "*saudades,*" and that word alone evokes a feeling of nostalgia, longing, yearning, love, and gratitude. *Saudades* is what you feel when you suddenly stumble upon a forgotten memento from your childhood, or a smell that transports you to a specific moment in your life, or a particular taste, and you close your eyes and savor it.

When Elias finished reading the letter, they all clapped and he handed me both letters. Then he presented me with a gift wrapped in red paper with the words "For Irene" written on it. I opened it, and out came two lovely, shiny *capulanas*, the beautiful textiles of Mozambique, black with a pattern that looked like drops or leaves in a faded cream color. Zulmira, standing next to me, took them and started dressing me as tradition holds. She wrapped the first one around my waist and the second one on my head. The students roared with claps, laughter and joy, and following this, took pictures with me individually.

"Teacher, these capulanas suit you very well!" said Cris.

"You are a Mozambican woman!" said Lizete.

Following the pictures, Elias handed me a champagne bottle and asked me to open it.

"My dear students, I love you so much, I'm going to miss you immensely when I leave. I will never forget this beautiful celebration. You have given me so much happiness, and it's so rewarding to know that you have learned and that you have taken something with you from our lessons. Thank you for making this journey rewarding, meaningful, and unforgettable," I said, swallowing deeply after every sentence to keep myself from crying.

They clapped and we all came together for a massive group hug, where I became one entity, wrapping each other with our arms, holding the greatest gift: our friendship. We were the personification of uBuntu then, and time appeared to slow down.

Then the champagne cork popped out, and screams and claps were heard all around. I filled the cups and we cheered: to us, to our friendship, and to our reunion in the future. It was time to eat. We were hungry, for we devoured the entire pots of chicken, rice, and xima in silence, savoring every bite, licking our fingers with delight.

The party wouldn't have been complete without Elias playing his guitar. There were two guitars, and some other friends had joined our celebration. Crimildo, another one of my students, played too, and we embarked on a singing frenzy, raising our voices to existing tunes and songs, and making up our own lyrics.

That night we sang and danced and celebrated that we were alive. We danced, and danced, and danced, all through the night. We forgot time, we forgot place, we forgot there was a yesterday and a tomorrow. We danced as if we were following Pina Bausch's credo "Dance, dance, otherwise we are lost," as if our entire lives were dependent on that music and the movement of our bodies. We let go.

One by one, students started leaving. The survivors were Crimildo, Elias, and I; we were the last to leave the bar. We carried everything we had taken back to Elias' house. We walked on the empty street, in the dark night; only the light from the moon and the stars above guided us, and only the sound of the swaying palm trees could be heard other than our whispers. Elias carried a huge pot on his head filled with smaller pots, plates, spoons and cups, my bag around his body, and the guitar in his hand.

As quietly as we could, we left everything on the porch of his house, and Crimildo bid us farewell.

"I'll walk you home," Elias told me.

Macia was asleep, and we enjoyed the stillness and quietness of our surroundings. We stopped on our way and sat down for a few minutes to talk.

"Did you like the capulanas?" Elias asked me.

"Of course I did! I love them!" I replied.

"I chose them for you... I thought they really matched your skin," he laughed.

"I guessed you had chosen them. I know you were in charge of planning everything. I don't know how to thank you, Elias, you've done so much for me!" I said.

"*You* have done so much for me, Madame, for all of us. This is just a small gesture to show our appreciation for everything you've done. I wish there was more I could give you," Elias sighed. But then he smiled and continued, "You have changed me. Ever since I met you, I have become a better person, I just want you to know that."

I hugged him tightly and said, "Elias, you couldn't possibly give me anything better than what you've just told me. That means everything to me. The greatest gift is your friendship, and for that I thank you, from the bottom of my heart!"

"No, thank *you*! KHANIMAMBO!" he said loudly. We both laughed and resumed our walk to my house.

***

Elias had his guitar tied around his body when, like so many of my friends and students, he came on the afternoon of September 21st to the Missionary House to bid me farewell. There were lots of people around, and he seemed a bit uncomfortable. We were standing under the clothesline and he said, half whispering,

"There is a big hole in my heart."

"Why?" I asked him.

"Because you are leaving. I wish you could stay," and I saw that he swallowed his tears. I couldn't keep myself from crying.

"I will come back, Elias, I promise. You'll see. We'll be together again, and we'll always keep in touch," I said.

"Madame, I will miss you." We held hands; and, as he usually did, he pressed mine really hard, as if trying to transmit that sorrow he felt for my departure and that beautiful love we had cultivated with our friendship. I hugged him tightly, and he left. That was the last time I saw him.

***

Elias remains alive in my memory. In my heart he will always exist. For he was one of those human beings who roam this planet and leave an indelible mark. Our friendship stands as proof to that; his legacy continues to live on through me and the thousands he touched. I wrote the following letter to him while I was living in China in 2011, and my friends there encouraged me to send him a message by writing a letter and burning it--that way it would reach him. I did so and kept a copy of the letter as a reminder of that special moment and as a tribute to his life.

To my dear friend, Elias,

Elias, you taught me how to improvise songs while you played your guitar. You were such a talented musician. Together, we came up with the funniest and sweetest tunes. You loved my voice and always encouraged me to sing.

Elias, you taught me how to diagnose Tuberculosis by singling out Koch's bacillus in the microscope. You taught me how to diagnose malaria by looking for the plasmodium falciparum in the microscope--and you successfully diagnosed my malaria when I felt weak. Thanks to you, to your sharp diagnostic abilities, I'm alive and healthy today.

Elias, you brought happiness into my days. You liked to challenge ideas and we often engaged in debates and discussions about life, friendship, religion and politics.

Elias, you told me once that we should all walk barefoot, like monkeys, because our shoes isolated the earth's energy from our bodies, and that contact was so powerful that it could even cure diseases. Perhaps if you had done it, you would still be alive today.

Elias, you are everywhere in my diary, in my memories, in my pictures, in my heart.

Elias, your curious and clever nature brought you to my English classes, where you always excelled.

Elias, we shared our worries, our fears, our dreams. You were so great--you had so much potential. You were brilliant.

Elias, you loved to play chess, and although we always said we had to play, only once did we attempt a game, which was abruptly interrupted. Your life was an unfinished game of chess too. You had so many moves to make still, an important match to win. I was certain that in the end, you would win. I had faith in you.

Elias, you liked watching bad scary movies, and once we bought one together and watched it on my laptop under the shack we had as our classroom. We laughed and joked about it.

Elias, you were the best at your job, and most importantly, you loved what you did. You saved millions of lives. Everyone knew you.

Elias, you told me that I worked too much. You said that during the day, there should be a time to 'reflect'-- that's the word you used. You said, "You should work from 8am until 4 pm or 5pm, and then you need time to reflect, and then sleep."

Elias, I told you once you couldn't be selfish, because you wanted to spend every weekend together, and I said it was important to share our time with everybody.

Elias, I taught you about nutrition and healthy ways to improve your diet. I also taught you how to drink tea without sugar--an unthinkable task in Mozambique!

Elias, together we worked on several blood donation campaigns. You always said we were the best team, that we worked well together, that we were very efficient.

Elias, you told me I should study to be a lab technician just like you. You said, "you are very talented."

Elias, you were there for me in one of my weakest moments. You saw my tears, you held my hand, you comforted me.

Elias, you told me that I had changed your life, that you had become a better person thanks to me. I was happy to know that I also taught you something.

Elias, you were always the leader. You organized a surprise party for me from all the students. You prepared a delicious meal, and gave me beautiful capulanas.

Elias, you gave me a resistant blue mosquito net with insecticide, which I'm sure, saved me many times.

Elias, you always shared your food with me, and we would sit under the big mango tree at the hospital and eat it with our hands.

Elias, you gave Dona Anabela and I money when we worked in Pfuka so we could buy tomatoes, lettuce, onion and bread to have breakfast/lunch together.

Elias, you always wanted me to eat more, and you were happy to see me gain weight.

Elias, when I left, you said there was a huge hole in your heart. Now, there's one in mine, deeper than any hole I've ever had.

Elias, you had a daughter and a wife, and you loved them. Your daughter looks just like you.

Elias, you were strong, you never got sick, and when I said you needed to be careful, you reassured me that nothing would happen to you.

Elias, your untimely death hurts me so much. I hate malaria, I curse the day it was born in the world, and I curse the mosquito that bit you.

Elias, I'm sorry for the times we argued and got angry at each other.

Elias, you always protected me. You assured me that nothing bad would ever happen to me, and I felt safe with you.

Elias, today is one of the saddest days in my life. It's very hard for me to find consolation, but I'm trying to find it in our pictures, our memories and the joy that meeting you brought into my life.

Elias, you gave me the greatest gift anyone in this world could ever hope for: friendship.

Thank you.

Your friend forever,

Irene Greaves

In an often grueling environment, Elias and I cultivated this beautiful friendship filled with joy and laughter, hope and strength. Our exchange of ideas and knowledge led us to a mutual enrichment, because our love was based on respect and trust, and we cultivated it with patience, communication, empathy, and care. And that love explains how two people from entire different backgrounds can love each other so deeply and truly regardless of their differences.

Friends embrace those differences and rejoice in them, learn from them, and grow from them. Is there a better example of choosing to love? I can assert that there is no better way to express love as a choice than through friendship; and that explains why obvious differences that set us apart never divided us but, rather, enhanced our friendship. Because we learned and shared our experiences, respected and accepted each other. That is love.

A *Sevillana* song I used to dance to says, *"Algo se muere en el alma cuando un amigo se va,* something dies in the soul when a friend leaves." If you think about the cycle of nature--death, life, death, life, death, life...--you realize it becomes a cycle of rebirth. So even the death that our soul suffers when a friend ceases to exist, results in rebirth, in a new form of life--of remembrance, if you will. The vacuum and emptiness that is left with the death of a friend will eventually be filled with the love that comes from all the memories and experiences shared together. Love becomes the rebirth that fills the hole in our soul the death of our departed friend has created.

While I lived in Mozambique, I attended more funerals than I ever had in my life, and almost every day I learned about the death of someone who was somehow connected to me. Elias was not my only friend who passed away after I left Mozambique. Through the contemplation of death, I found love, which led me to peace.

What is Lovescaping?

We see and hear it all around us; from popular songs such as "All You Need is Love," "Love is in the Air," or "I Will Always Love You," to inspirational quotes and messages on social media, speeches, movies, TV shows, and books, urging us to love ourselves and love others. Our society is obsessed with love--unfortunately though, I would argue that the obsession is with a superficial and inaccurate idea of love. And until we take love seriously and understand what it truly means to love, our society will not evolve.

Love has been co-opted. I am not sure when or how this happened, but our society has greatly distorted what it means to love. Living in an era of mass connectivity (and yet mass disconnection), mass disposability, and a mass desire for instant-gratification has greatly contributed to the distortion that love has suffered. Love is what binds our humanity together; it's what all human beings yearn to feel; and the lack of it is the root cause of all the affliction in our world. A society based on the principles of love that practices love in action has no room for discrimination, fear, hatred, aggression, racism, xenophobia, or any other form of violence and oppression. I call these the antitheses of love.

"But some people kill for love," I hear as a response to counter my assertion.

My answer is simple: *That* is not love.

Much of the problem surrounding the lack of serious discussion on the topic of love stems from the fact that we do not have a working definition of it, and perhaps the notion we do have of it dangerously derives from over-simplified, idealized, and sentimentalized depictions of mainly romantic love in our popular culture. bell hooks has addressed this issue in a meaningful and insightful way, and her writing has been a constant source of hope and inspiration to me. She has been raising many of the questions and issues I raise here for many years, particularly regarding the incorrect assumption that we will instinctively know how to love. Her book, *all about love,* helped me name and understand many of the thoughts and feelings I could not express before, and encouraged me to move forward with Lovescaping.

Where do we learn how to love? How do we know what love is? How is our capacity to love shaped and affected by the environment we are raised in? Love is an essential condition not only for our survival, but for our ability to thrive and live nurturing, fulfilling and healthy lives. I believe that there is a way for us to learn how to love. This is precisely what Lovescaping seeks to accomplish: to create the right environment for us to practice love in action.

Practicing love in action demands intentionality and purposefulness. Love does not just happen--it is like a seed that needs to be planted and nurtured in order to bloom. Lovescaping consists of a number of values and actions, that I term pillars, without which love cannot exist.

I like to think about the pillars of Lovescaping in three different analogies. The first is that they form the pillars of a temple: a temple can still stand even if some of its pillars have been broken or damaged, however the structure becomes unstable and prone to damage and collapse. Practicing our pillars is equivalent to maintaining a strong and stable temple. Our current society is a temple about to shatter into a million pieces, and the lone pillar that keeps it standing is hope. Once hope is broken, what's left of the temple will crumble. We can never let this happen.

The second analogy is that they are puzzle pieces. A puzzle is made up of different pieces that fit together to make a shape, show an image, or reveal a message. Even if we can make sense of the shape or theme of the puzzle once a number of pieces are in place, the puzzle is still incomplete without all its pieces. The pillars are the puzzle pieces, and through the practice of each of them, we join them together to ultimately reveal the complete power of Lovescaping.

The third and final analogy is that the pillars are instruments in an orchestra. An orchestra is one of my favorite examples of the whole being greater than the sum of its parts. We can think of every pillar as an instrument, and each one must be played at the right time and in the right rhythm to produce the graceful, harmonious sounds of the symphony.

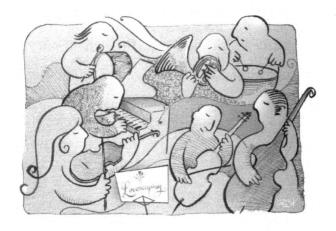

If we think of Lovescaping as an orchestra, then its fifteen pillars constitute fifteen instruments, and it takes continuous practice on behalf of the musicians to tune their instruments, play at the same beat, coordinate their actions, and achieve mastery as a team. Lovescaping creates the most beautiful symphony in the world; and if we want to hear it, we must learn to play each one of its instruments.

Almost every day, family members and friends share articles with me about how most jobs will become obsolete in the next decade. These pieces urge us to reconsider our studies: "If you are studying law, stop this instant!" one recently warned. Artificial intelligence will replace a high percentage of human jobs in the very near future, and this will force us to reconsider how our societies function. Indeed, it is frightening to think about the automated future--what will human beings do if there is no need for them to work? I will not attempt to address what specific skills the workforce will need or not need in the future, but I will stress the absolute urgency for love.

No matter what that society in the future looks like, one need remains a priority: the need to learn how to love. Robots and machines may take over our daily tasks, but no issue is more important, more urgent and more timely than learning how to love. We must be equipped with the greatest power of all, the power for which there is no rival: the power of love. I dream of a world in which human beings collectively and intentionally practice Lovescaping. This is my hope, and I shall fight for it with all my might, as long as I remain on this Earth.

Lovescaping introduces a new paradigm, a new point of view so imperative to bringing forth the change that we need in the world. Let me give you a simple definition before I elaborate on each of the pillars:

Lovescaping is practicing love in action through the active and intentional engagement of its fifteen pillars.

This work starts with ourselves. My hope is that by acknowledging the enormity of the gap that exists between theory and practice, empty words and action, we will begin to act in a congruent manner and begin to love ourselves and others. This is the work of my life, based on my experiences as a human being and in my role as an educator, teaching in different contexts with a methodology and a pedagogy that has always been informed by and with love.

Some of the complexities surrounding the topic of love include what is perceived as its abstract and intangible nature, although we all have an idea of what love means and what it should look like. Lovescaping is constituted by fifteen essential pillars, without which love cannot exist:

Respect	Trust	Vulnerability
Care	Patience	Solidarity
Honesty	Compassion	Hope
Communication	Liberation	Gratitude
Empathy	Humility	Forgiveness

Love is not a simplistic concept; all of these pillars are necessary for its realization and actualization. Love cannot exist without each pillar being practiced. This is why love is not easy: it takes place in a space where we cultivate *all* of these pillars. There is no hierarchy for these practices; they feed off and build upon each other--they cannot exist alone. I like to show them visually in the shape of a circle. Life is a cycle, and expressing love in terms of a circle shows it ever-continuing. It is a work in progress, a journey that is constantly renewed. In this regard, love acts as a symbol of infinite and boundless power:

In the discourse of love we need a conception of community, for-the-greater-good, and uBuntu. An individual does not and cannot live in alienation from others. The overemphasis on individualism is one of the greatest flaws in our current political and social systems, and the cause of many of today's world problems. If we were to embrace a Lovescaping way of life in which my well-being depends on your well-being and the well-being of all of those that surround us, our world would certainly be a very different place.

With a system built upon the pillars of Lovescaping we have the potential to change the world.

Intentionality and Purposefulness

I would like to emphasize the importance of intentionality and purposefulness in the practice of Lovescaping. To be intentional means making a conscious decision to practice the pillars of Lovescaping, to be fully aware that we are making *a choice* when practicing love. If we have a plant at home, we need to be intentional about looking after it, watering it, making sure it gets enough sunlight, nutrients, etc. We don't expect it to survive if we don't make an intentional effort to care for it. The same applies to love: we can't just assume love will survive without us taking an intentional and active role in practicing it.

To be purposeful means acting towards our goal to become Lovescapers. The purpose of Lovescaping is for every human being to practice love in action, and we must always remember this goal. We should continually strive towards it, and never lose sight of it, even in the hardest and darkest moments of our lives. We must wrap this purposefulness around the pillar of hope, since that will give us the strength we need to get through the most difficult times.

Self-Awareness

Self-awareness is a term that has become massively popular in the recent years. The problem when certain words or terms become "buzzwords" is that they lose their actual value because people throw them around left and right without practicing them. This happens with many words, and it has happened to love. Practicing Lovescaping intentionally and purposefully requires us to actually be, or to become, self-aware, not just to throw the term around.

Being self-aware means looking at ourselves with a critical and introspective lens in order to evaluate our own thoughts, behaviors and actions. It means being able to self-reflect and self-assess ourselves in any given situation. As the word implies, it means being *aware* of our own selves and everything that comes with them--who we are, where we come from, and why we think and act the way we do. As we explore the pillars of Lovescaping, you will realize how practicing each pillar will help us become self-aware.

Self-awareness also allows us to fill the gap that exists between theory and practice. Most people know what all the pillars of Lovescaping mean, but do their actions reflect the same? It is easy to say "I know what respect is," but are you actually *being* respectful? Are you actually *being* empathic? Through intentionality and self-awareness, we will realize that it is much easier to talk than it is to act. Lovescaping is not concerned with just defining these pillars, it is about making the actions involved in each one a conscious, regular practice. Only then, can love truly exist.

The Yellow Road

If I gave you the following options, which one would you choose?

There are two roads to get to your destination. The blue road is easy and will get you there faster, but your journey will be lonely. You will experience fleeting pleasures, fleeting emotions, but no real connection with anyone. There will be no growth, no lessons learned, no joy or sadness, nothing--just an empty road with you in it. The yellow road is hard, with plenty of obstacles along the way. During the journey you will stumble, you will fall, you will crawl, you will walk, you will run, you will learn, you will grow, you will suffer, and you will experience joy. You will meet many people along the way and learn to connect with each one of them. You will become wise. You will reach your destination later, but you will have accomplished the most difficult task of all: you will have learned how to love.

Yes, this is a rhetorical question, but it is important to recognize that we often choose to take the blue road because it is easier. I do not intend to judge the people who choose to take the blue road; I have at certain times in my life also chosen it because it has offered some protection--a shield from feeling. The blue road can serve as a defense mechanism to shield ourselves from many emotions, some that feel too painful to endure. When we Lovescape, we choose to take the yellow road, which is hard, but so much more worthwhile. Because when we choose to love, we shall be loved in return.

Two crucial points here might go against popular beliefs or might seem counterintuitive, but they are fundamental to the practice of Lovescaping. The first point is that it is difficult to practice love, and we have to work very hard for it. The second point is that, in the act of loving others, we also begin to develop self-love. It is true that nurturing self-love is necessary for us to love others. However, the reality is we don't develop self-love in a vacuum, meaning, we don't just wave a magic wand and tell ourselves "I love myself," and *voilá!* that's it (if only it were that easy, right?). We are social beings and we live in a society where the people who surround us impact how we view and what we believe about ourselves. A lot of our self-worth and self-value is derived from our interactions with other people, the sort of relationships we create and the environments we are a part of. The exceptional quality about love is that it is contagious: the more love we receive, the more love we give, and the more self-love we develop. Essentially, the act of loving someone helps you develop self-love, which in turns helps you love others, and so forth, the cycle continues. This is the sort of virtuous cycle that occurs when we let love permeate our lives.

Un-learning

Often times, in order to master something, we have to un-learn it first. We have all had exposure to love in some form or another, maybe it's the love we received from our mother, our father, our grandparents, our friends, our teachers, our spouses... I do not intend to say that these manifestations or forms of love are not valid, or wrong. Everybody is different and therefore expresses love in different ways. However, I do want to encourage you to embrace Lovescaping, and in doing so, challenge you to perhaps un-learn some things you have learned in regards to love, practices that stand in direct contrast to many of our pillars. The good news is that the human brain has the ability to learn and un-learn, to grow and change, no matter how old we are. I hope that as you read these pages, you look deep inside yourself and question some of the ways in which you have shown love or others have shown love to you. I encourage you to un-learn wherever necessary so that you can fully and openly learn to Lovescape.

So let's explore each one of Lovescaping's pillars. Then I'll share my experience with Lovescaping in education and some inspiring examples of other practitioners' work and show you how you can put these pillars in action.

Let's start Lovescaping!

The Pillars of Lovescaping

Respect

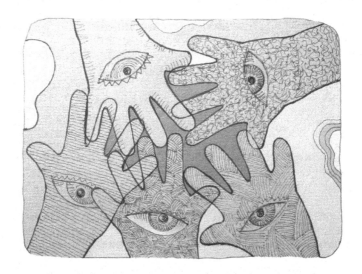

Respect means acknowledging another person's existence, much as we acknowledge our own, treating ourselves and others with the dignity that we all deserve as human beings. It entails giving value, listening, and recognizing another person's voice, point of view, and lived experiences. In order to love, we need to feel a sense of deep respect and admiration for the people and the world around us. When we nurture respect, we learn to listen to different points of view, to tolerate and accept differences, and to value diversity based on that mutual sense of validation for who we are. Having respect for humanity is necessary for love to be cultivated in our world.

We practice respect by recognizing the inherent value that every human being has for the mere reason of existing. No matter how different we are, we all share one common bond: we belong to the human race. For that reason alone, we are each worthy of respect. Respect starts with the act of listening and acknowledging that every person has a voice, that every person's experiences inform who they are and how they see the world. Respect is not about agreeing or disagreeing with people, it's not even about *liking* them. Respect is about treating every human being in a way that is dignifying. This can be done by something as simple as making eye contact with the person we are engaging with, by not interrupting while she is speaking, by keeping a tone of voice that doesn't devolve into yelling or cursing, by being mindful about the words we use, or by saying "please," and "thank you," among other respectful actions.

Practicing respect also involves honoring the individuality and uniqueness of every human being. It means not looking down on others, valuing their privacy and their space, understanding that there is a time and a place for everything, and respecting the space that exists between each one of us. This space that I am referring to is both literal and figurative, since it involves our actual physical space (i.e., our bodies), and the metaphoric space (i.e., our individuality, our thoughts), both of which need to be respected.

Respect is often shown through our body language. It is so easy to communicate nonverbally that "you matter" and also that "you don't matter." Have you ever felt disrespected? Think about the actions of the person who made you feel disrespected-- was it his tone of voice? His body language? The words he used? There are many ways in which we knowingly or unknowingly disrespect others. What should you do if someone disrespects you?

For this and many questions that are in the same vein with regards to the other pillars, my answer is similar: respect them in return. What is the difference between you and that person if you disrespect him back? Where do we put an end to vicious cycles that are formed by repeating a behavior that is destructive? Be the better person and lead by example. This is easier said than done, and of course there will be moments when we won't be able to contain ourselves, when we may curse and scream and say hurtful things. After all, we are only human. But that is why we have forgiveness and humility as two of our other pillars. We can rely on them when we are pushed beyond the limits of our ability to be as respectful as we want to be.

Love is nurtured with respect.

Care

Caring means giving time and attention to and looking after things or people that matter to us with kindness and affection. It means we attach importance to another person's well-being and we invest the time it takes to nurture a relationship. We show that we care about others by being consistent, reliable, and trustworthy. We show up, we are there to support in the good times and the bad times, and we recognize that the most valuable resource we have--the most precious gift we can give to show that we care--is our time. If you want to find out who you care most about, just look at the time that you spend with each one of those people; similarly, if you want to know what you care about most, look at the time you spend on each of your endeavors.

When we care for the well-being of others, we are good observers and notice when someone is not doing well. We offer our help, whether that comes in the form of a hug, advice, or a listening ear. Caring about others helps us develop our sense of altruism and selflessness, along with our ability to empathize. As with all the pillars of Lovescaping, care also starts with us: it is crucial for us to practice self-care in order for us to care for others. How we look after our health, how well we nurture our mental health, how we treat our bodies, what sort of dialogue we have with ourselves: all these impact our ability to care.

Small acts of kindness go a long way in showing others we care about them. We often underestimate the effect that a greeting, a message, a compliment, or a gesture can have on someone. With something as simple as telling our neighbor, "Have a wonderful day," to helping an elderly person cross the street, to sending a text message to a friend letting her know that we are thinking of her, to asking follow-up questions when people tell us something that matters to them, we are saying, "*I notice you, I value you, I care about you.*" Through kindness, we show appreciation for the people we care about, and we nurture a safe and positive environment where love thrives.

When we are babies, our parents take care of us because we are unable to care for ourselves. Once we grow older and learn to take care of ourselves we also begin to develop the ability to care for others. But if somewhere along the way we lose track of our own self-care, it can become very difficult to care about others. However, given the virtuous cycle we discussed earlier, somebody's caring actions towards you can aid you in regaining your own self-care, which in turn allows you to care for others. And so the chain goes on, and one by one, we begin to change people's behaviors so that they learn to take care of themselves and the people around them.

Love is nurtured with caring actions.

Honesty

Honesty means being truthful, open, and transparent. Honesty requires high degrees of vulnerability and trust. As honesty develops, the environment becomes conducive to sincere and open conversations. Honesty means speaking our truth to others, expressing our feelings, emotions, fears, dreams, doubts, and experiences. Honesty allows us to build authentic relationships based on our true selves. Being honest can be very difficult, it can even hurt at times, but it is necessary to build a solid relationship based on truth and trust.

Do you remember when you first told a lie? From a young age we learn to tell lies mainly for two reasons: to get what we want, and from fear (usually of being punished). In some ways, lying can become a coping or even a survival mechanism, since fear is one of the most effective inhibitors of honesty. However, if we adopt Lovescaping as a way of life, fear vanishes, since it is one of the antitheses of love. Fear is one of the most effective ways to control, coerce, and manipulate people, and much of the history of humanity is a history of fear. It takes a lot of un-learning to transition from fear to love and practicing honesty alongside learning to be vulnerable and to trust is the first step in that direction.

As with every single pillar, honesty begins with ourselves. How many times have you felt like you've been wearing a mask to hide your true self? How many times have you lied out of fear of what others would think? How many times have you lied to yourself because it is too painful to admit the truth? Being honest with ourselves forces us to make alignments in our lives between what we hold to be true and how we are acting towards it. Embracing honesty also provides a sense of liberation, relief, and empowerment; it feels like a weight is taken off your shoulders.

Love is nurtured with honesty.

Communication

Communication is like a dance where dancers follow the rhythm of the music together, where they twirl and turn, glide and stride, jump and dip, where no words are spoken, but their bodies move harmoniously, each following the other's movements, communicating silently in a *seemingly* effortless way. Communication, like dance, is an art. In order for us to perfect it, we must practice it industriously, learn to read body language, to pick up subtleties in the tone, in the choice of words used, in what is said and what isn't said, and in the silences. Communication entails transmitting our thoughts, feelings, and emotions through different mediums.

We communicate constantly, exchanging information, and addressing each other in verbal and non-verbal ways. We often hear that communication is the basis of any relationship, and indeed, a relationship cannot exist without communication. Our ability to communicate allows us to survive, grow, and develop. From the moment we are born, we learn to express our needs with our signature communicative action: crying. As we grow older, we start learning how to use words to express our feelings and emotions, and the more vocabulary we gain, the better equipped we become to transmit our ideas, resolve conflict, and think about and learn new concepts.

The amount, the frequency and the way in which we communicate all impact our ability to build a relationship. Body language is worth a thousand words: it transmits very clear and powerful messages. If the person you are talking to is not making eye contact with you, is slouching on a chair, or is holding his head in his hand, he sends a very clear message, "I am bored/uninterested." It is crucial to be aware of what messages we are sending with our body language so that we don't hurt or offend the people we are communicating with. Remember, if we are practicing respect, we use our body language to show that we are listening and that we are engaged, letting the person we are communicating with know that we respect him.

Words are like fire. They are an essential part of our lives--necessary for our survival--but they are also ruthless, destructive, and unforgiving if left unattended. The choice of words we use to express what we think and how we feel carries enormous weight and has enormous consequences. Words have the ability to lift, to heal, and to empower, and at the same time the ability to hurt, to degrade, and to disempower. Sometimes, we unintentionally use words that cause great pain, and we have no idea how much they can haunt another person's life forever. We might have the best intentions at heart, but we don't realize that the words we are using are having the opposite effect of our intended purpose.

It takes a lot of self-awareness and empathy to realize what effect our words are having on another person. Ask yourself, "How would I feel if someone said that to me?" and "How might what I'm about to say negatively impact the other person?" By taking a moment to reflect about the power our words carry, we might be able to prevent unintentionally hurting someone's feelings. However, if the harm has been done already, we still have the ability to heal those wounds, through our caring actions, our choice of words in the future, and, if needed, one of our other pillars: forgiveness.

Dialogue is one of the most important elements of communication. Dialogue means engaging in a reciprocal communicative action that leads to an exchange of ideas, listening, understanding, discussing, reflecting, engaging, and ultimately creating new forms of knowledge, new ways of looking at the world, of finding solutions to problems and creating meaningful insight. When we engage in dialogue, we are validating and respecting another person's viewpoint, even if we don't agree with it. In fact, engaging through dialogue helps us build empathy because we get to listen to, know, and ultimately understand another person.

Silence is also a form of communication. What we choose to say matters as much as what we choose *not* to say. Silence, like words, has the power to hurt and the power to heal. Sometimes, remaining silent can be the wisest and best thing to do in a given situation. While we are listening to someone we should remain silent and try not to interrupt unless absolutely necessary. Sustaining silence after words have been spoken can often be the most appropriate response in situations where there really isn't much to say, where a person just needs to express herself, but is not seeking an opinion. In these situations, our mere presence and our silence communicates infinitely more than any words could. As we grow older, we begin to identify these situations and to express the wisdom that comes with silence. Practicing empathy is another effective way to sustain silence.

On the flip side, silence can also hurt. Choosing to remain silent in a situation that requires us to speak up makes us complicit. What sort of situations require us to raise our voices? Whenever we find ourselves in the presence of any form of violence and oppression-- the antitheses of love--we need to raise our voices and denounce whatever injustice we are witnessing. It takes much courage to speak up against oppression, but once we learn to practice honesty, compassion, and solidarity and understand the importance of liberation, we realize that there is no room for silence in the presence of abuse and violence.

Lack of communication is often the number one cause of conflict in any type of relationship. It is ironic that we live in an era of mass communication, yet we still fail to communicate clearly and effectively. One of the biggest inhibitors of communication is our assumptions. We assume that people will know how we feel, what we think, or what we want, because we expect them to, or because we believe they already know. Our failure to communicate directly, coherently and without reservation results in people making assumptions all the time. This turns into a vicious cycle whereby we become afraid to ask or say something, which ultimately results in conflict because there is a misalignment between the perceived and actual need in a given situation. Once we suspend all assumptions, we realize that in order for our needs to be met, there is no other choice but to communicate clearly, openly, honestly, and specifically.

Love happens through communication--our loving actions are indeed a form of communication. We could even make the argument that each one of Lovescaping's pillars is a form of communication that involves both words and actions. The best type of communication is the one in which our actions are congruent with what our words are saying.

Love is nurtured with communication.

Empathy

Empathy means being able to place ourselves in other people's shoes in order to understand them. This means having the ability to see and feel the world as if we were the other person. Psychologist Carl Rogers' definition of empathy is "a way to perceive the internal frame of reference of another with accuracy, and with the emotional components and meanings which pertain thereto, as if one were the other person, but without ever losing the 'as if' condition." I like this definition because it emphasizes the 'as if' component, which is crucial to understanding how empathy works. It would be impossible to feel exactly what another person is feeling, even if she is undergoing a situation that we have already experienced because everybody reacts and feels differently.

However, the beauty of empathy is that it allows us to cultivate perspective-taking, to practice it, and to use the other person's lens to get as close as we can to feeling what she feels. This is one of the most important and powerful expressions of love because it leads to the wholehearted understanding of a person's feelings. The study of empathy in the educational context has been around for a while now, and it has recently become more popular as our society wakes up to understanding the importance of teaching it.

Advances in neuroscience have also shed light on the nature of empathy on our brains. The groundbreaking work of the English clinical psychologist Dr. Simon Baron-Cohen clearly shows that there is a specific place for empathy in our brains that can be observed and measured when activated, which he calls the empathy circuit. Antisocial and psychopathic behavior can be understood by looking at brains that lack empathy. Dr. Baron-Cohen explains that there are two components to empathy just as we know there are two sides of the brain: the cognitive, the left side of the brain, represents the ability to put yourself in others' shoes; and the affective, the right side of the brain, represents the ability to respond to what someone else is feeling or thinking.

His research into the minds of psychopaths and serial killers shows that many of them do have cognitive empathy. They are able to connect with their victims at the cognitive level. However, they clearly lack affective empathy, which prevents them from responding to the feelings of others. And that is why they feel no remorse. Dr. Baron-Cohen's research shows that even though there are genetic and biological factors that contribute to a person's ability to feel—or not feel-- empathy, environmental (or nurture) factors are crucial in its development. This is a hopeful message, one that allows us to say with confidence: we can learn to empathize.

It is easier to be empathic when a part of us identifies with the other, or at least feels with and for the other. But the point of empathy is to open our minds and hearts to all different ways of looking and understanding the world. Choosing to love and practicing empathy means doing it *even*, and perhaps most importantly, with people we disagree with. Otherwise, how do we break bigotry cycles? We need to open our hearts and understand a person through *his* lens if we want to have an open dialogue where we attempt to find common ground and give validity and value to his lived experiences. How can we expect others to listen to us if we are unwilling to listen to them? Empathy starts with us.

How then, can we learn to become empathic?

The Power of Story

Many people have told me that you can't really understand, or change, or take somebody else's perspective until you have actually gone through the same or similar situation. I disagree with this notion, precisely because of empathy. The whole point of empathy is to be able to step into somebody else's world, however familiar or unfamiliar it might be. How do we do that? Simply, by listening to someone's story. Every human being has a story. When we open our hearts to truly listen, we experience the transformative potential of empathy. Unfortunately, it is much easier for us to take the shortcut of labeling others based on our beliefs, stereotypes, assumptions, or rumors, and exclude them. In other words, it's easier to dismiss a person than it is to try to understand him.

Remember, this work is difficult. But the mere act of being open to listening to somebody else's story is half the battle. And by listening I mean hearing or reading their words with the intent to understand, not with the intent to respond or make judgment calls. I have witnessed time after time how a person's opinion about an issue changed after being open to listening to someone's story. When we truly listen, we step into someone else's world, and we automatically have to ask, "What would I have done in that situation?" This exercise is also incredibly humbling if done properly. Once we suspend judgment we realize that we are all imperfect human beings doing the best we can with what we have at our disposal.

As I mentioned previously, we can learn to sustain silence by practicing empathy since rarely is there a need for words when we are being empathic. The key to empathy is listening, tuning in, and absorbing everything another person is saying, not with the intent to respond, but with the intent to understand. During that silent moment, we are acknowledging that you are there to listen and support; and more often than not, a hug, a smile, or a nod go a long way in showing the person that we understand, we care.

Unless specifically solicited by the person talking, we shouldn't try to give advice or reply with a story of how that happened to us in the past. There is a time and a place to exchange experiences, but while we are practicing empathy, it is time to listen. Sustaining silence is the best response.

Love is nurtured with empathy.

Trust

Trust is the ability to believe sincerely in someone or something. It requires us to be vulnerable and honest and to let go of fear. It means finding support and being able to count on that support-- like being blindfolded and letting someone guide you. Without looking at the path ahead, you know that you are going to get to where you need to go because you trust the person who is guiding you. Developing trust takes time, like most of Lovescaping's pillars, it is not something that occurs overnight, it needs to be cultivated and cared for, and it requires a mutual covenant by which we become trusting and trustworthy.

Trust is the inevitable consequence of being honest, caring, vulnerable, and communicative. We learn to trust people when they show us they are trustworthy: they care about us; they are honest and vulnerable, and they are able to show it. Trust is earned over time, and it is something we choose to give once a person has shown that they are worthy of it. Without trust, no relationship can flourish, since it is the pillar that allows us to believe in others wholeheartedly.

Disappointment is one of the worst feelings we experience when trust is broken. How crushing is it to realize that someone you trusted has cheated you? Trust is one of the hardest pillars to rebuild once it's been broken, because it is very painful to come to grips with the reality that something you spent years developing is suddenly destroyed. It's not impossible to rebuild trust, but it takes a lot of time and a lot of work. We all make mistakes, and our actions have consequences. We can turn to empathy and try to understand why that trust was broken, and through forgiveness, begin the healing process to rebuild it together.

Love is nurtured with trust.

Patience

Patience means having the skill to allow for the necessary time to pass in order for things to develop and start taking their course, without becoming agitated, or upset, or losing our temper. Patience is very closely linked to time, and to the recognition that most things that are important in this world require time. It takes time to develop trust, to learn, to understand, and ultimately to love. In this fast-changing and fast-moving world we have often forgotten the importance and the value of being patient. Our desire for instant gratification has left no room for patience, no room for valuing the time that it takes to make complex and meaningful things work.

Patience is highly overlooked or underrated, and in some cases even cast under a negative light and seen as a weakness, a waste of time, a useless skill. In a way, patience doesn't match the sort of lifestyle that we champion in the twenty-first century, where faster is *always* better. We need time to build relationships, to trust, to communicate, to learn how to be empathic-- none of these things happen overnight, and we need to be patient in their practice if we want to do them well. Patience is necessary for us if we are to learn how to love.

Having patience allows us to *reflect* on our experiences, our actions and our words. The ability to reflect and self-reflect are crucial in becoming more self-aware individuals. And being able to identify and recognize our strengths, weaknesses, and areas of growth are crucial in exercising all pillars of

Lovescaping. When we reflect, we are practicing patience because we are making the necessary time to think deeply and introspectively about our lives. Mindfulness is another excellent way to practice patience, since it requires us to take the time to be fully present.

We often seek standardized solutions and one-size-fits-all models to solve complex societal issues. These solutions lack patience, for they don't take into consideration the time that is required for meaningful and loving work to thrive. The most valuable thing we can give to anyone is our time, because ultimately it is the time we invest in building relationships, trust, and love that really matters. Yes, funds are needed to carry out projects and to invest in resources, but what can money do if nobody is willing to dedicate their time to collaborate and work together?

Love is nurtured with patience.

Compassion

Having compassion means being able to share other people's suffering and feel *with* them. It means not remaining indifferent to the world's sorrows and showing genuine care for what others are experiencing. Being compassionate helps alleviate the suffering of those around us because we share it collectively; it brings us together in a display of solidarity, and it shows that we care. Compassion is at the core of our humanity, since every human being suffers, and it is both powerful and humbling to share this experience together. When we extend our compassion to others we are letting them know that they are not alone in their suffering, that we are there to support and, if possible, take action.

It is easy to lose our compassion in extreme situations of war, rampant poverty, famine, or violence. One of the most defining aspects of human beings is our ability to get used to *anything*. It is our survival instinct that allows us to grow accustomed to the most inhumane conditions, where horrific acts become so commonplace that we almost become immune to them. If a society spirals into a humanitarian crisis where basic needs are unmet, it becomes increasingly easy to lose our compassion in order to survive. When people are in survival mode, hungry, and hopeless, it is easy to lose our humanity. The de-humanization begins with our own loss of compassion, and we might discover that we are capable of doing things we never thought we could do. Our basic needs must be met in order for us to practice compassion.

Lovescaping as a societal practice would prevent humanitarian crises to develop, but we are not there yet. In the meantime, it is important to acknowledge and understand the circumstances and situations that can lead to the de-humanization of an individual. When our well-being is tied to that of others, our compassion usually leads to action, to change; compassion can indeed be the catalyst that breaks the cycle of violence and oppression. It humanizes and inspires us to strive towards empathy and solidarity, nurturing our soul and illuminating the path towards Lovescaping.

Love is nurtured with compassion.

Liberation

Love is liberating, which means it sets free. Love is both an expression of freedom and a vehicle to achieve it. We cultivate liberation through our actions of love, because we learn to respect each other's humanity and we are constantly engaged in the practice of liberation. The act of loving is in itself an act of freedom, because it has no boundaries, and it knows no oppression. Educating as an act of love--with love, for love and through love--is an expression of freedom, since it liberates the soul, the mind, the heart, and the body of those involved in its praxis.

Love removes all barriers standing in the way of freedom. To truly love, we have to let go of all the chains that bind us, that scare us, that abuse us, that oppress us, that annihilate the possibility of dreaming, of having a vision, of having faith. Love has a transformative power because it instills hope, trust, and worthiness. I have witnessed the remarkable transformation that people undergo when they understand they are loved and suddenly begin to feel worthy. Then, the entire world opens up to them-- they start dreaming, believing, and having a vision for the future.

The pillar of liberation stands contrary to popular renditions of love as possessive, jealous, and controlling. Love liberates because it trusts, it is secure, and it sets the beloved free. In the practice of love, we respect the individuality and freedom of every human being, and we learn two important lessons. First, your liberation is tied to mine, because we are all inextricably connected. Until every single human being is free, we are not free. And second, our freedom comes with great responsibility to practice it alongside the other pillars of Lovescaping, since this will ensure that we do not misuse our own freedom and harm others.

Love is nurtured through liberation.

Humility

Being humble means recognizing the limitations of our own knowledge and existence as human beings. It means having the ability to acknowledge that we do not own the Truth and that, in fact, there is no truth with a capital T. At any given point, we can realize, learn or see that something we deemed right or true, is not. Just consider how much our world has changed in the last century. Our life expectancy has almost doubled thanks to breakthroughs in science and medicine. We take it for granted now, but a hundred years ago, we hadn't discovered penicillin, and people would die of bacterial infections that today we treat in a heartbeat. Consider how easy it is for us to travel nowadays and move around from one continent to the next by taking a flight, but a mere four hundred years ago we were still mapping our planet. Just consider how much knowledge we have acquired in the last few years and how it has helped us understand aspects of our own existence, from the makeup of our DNA, to the stars and galaxies beyond our planet. Think about how much we *don't know* yet.

Humility allows us to bear these realizations, not with reluctance or disappointment, but with an open heart. In other words, being humble means being aware of our own mortal existence, and approaching situations with an attitude that shows that in the end, we do not really know: we are just attempting to discover, to learn, and to grow.

Humility allows us to listen to others, to question our own biases, thoughts and beliefs, and it opens the path to nurture empathy. If we do not practice humility, we believe that there is only one right lens through which to view the world: our own. This can ultimately result in prejudice, judgement, intolerance, hatred, and the de-humanization of certain people.

A humble person understands that she is not above or below others, but sees herself as a human being on the same plain as all others, just different. If we stripped ourselves from all the constructs we have created to separate and divide us, if we looked at our bare selves, we would see that we are more similar than we are different. A humble person recognizes that her worldview is very much informed by her lived experiences, and the same goes for everybody else. A humble person listens and values others, and is open to change.

Humility begins with recognition. Recognizing that our beliefs and thoughts are shaped by the environment we are born into. So as an exercise, try the following: Instead of saying or thinking, "My beliefs are right, and yours are wrong," try "My beliefs are different from yours." Notice there is no judgement call of right or wrong in the second statement. Instead of saying or thinking, "I know," try "I don't know." Try imagining how different your life would be if you had been born in a completely different place than the one you are in... stop and think for a moment, "Would I be the same? Would I think the same? Would I have the same beliefs?'"

There are so many factors that influence how we think and who we become, and it's important to recognize that if we had been born in a completely different setting, we would see the world in very different ways. So why should we deem *our way*, the *right way*? Why aren't people who live on the other side of the world *right*? This leads us to the humbling conclusion: *nobody owns the truth.*

An incredibly humbling exercise that I often undertake is thinking big picture. Try this: close your eyes and feel your own presence. Think about where you are, your immediate surroundings; then zoom out and imagine seeing yourself from the sky; zoom out even more and imagine the shape of your city, your state, your country, and then imagine seeing your continent from space, like one of those amazing pictures of Earth that NASA takes. Proceed to zoom out as much as you can, see our planet among the other planets, see the sun, the moon, the stars. Zoom out further and see our galaxy.... Wow! We are but a tiny particle in this vast, infinite universe, in Carl Sagan's words, "a pale blue dot." In such a large universe, we are very miniscule, almost insignificant. This exercise is meant for us to put things into perspective and to recognize that as much as we like to think that we are so important we really are not.

Love is nurtured with humility.

Vulnerability

Shame researcher and bestselling author Dr. Brené Brown defines vulnerability as "uncertainty, risk, and emotional exposure." She debunks the greatest myth that surrounds vulnerability: it is a weakness. Dr. Brown argues that it is actually the opposite, and that most feelings we experience in our lives are at their core an act of vulnerability. In other words, vulnerability allows us to experience love. Life is filled with uncertainty and risk. For us to truly enjoy and embrace everything it has to offer, we have to be comfortable with not knowing, with risk, and with uncertainty, and we must expose ourselves emotionally in order to reveal our true selves to the world and *feel* entirely. When we learn to be vulnerable with one another, we begin developing trust, and we learn to be humble and to embrace the beauty of the unknown.

Our society does a very poor job of encouraging vulnerability, particularly for men. In the culture I was raised in, *machismo* is pervasive. Men are taught from an early age to "man up," which essentially equates to "Never show your emotions, and don't you dare cry-- that's what girls do!" (And of course there is no greater insult than being called a girl.) Somehow being vulnerable robs men of their manhood, and boys learn to put up an emotional barrier to conceal their feelings. Women are also taught to "man up" if they want to be taken seriously, and hence we have built a society that is deprived of vulnerability.

The consequences are serious. We are complex beings who experience a wide array of emotions and feelings, all of which are valid and need to be addressed and explored. Putting up an emotional wall denies our very human essence from flourishing, for how can we possibly grow and learn if we disregard what we feel? Remember the blue road? It is much easier to hide our emotions, to disengage and carry on with our lives in a rather automatic fashion. Being vulnerable is hard, and often painful, because it requires us to expose our whole selves to others, and doing that takes a colossal amount of courage and trust.

Fear is one of the biggest inhibitors of vulnerability-- both the fear of opening up and becoming vulnerable, and the fear of being exposed and then hurt after having been vulnerable. As I stated previously, the feeling of disappointment when someone you trusted betrays you is shattering, and trust is in itself an act of vulnerability. If we have been through this heartbreaking experience multiple times, we begin to distrust and close off, and with due reason! But by embracing Lovescaping as a way of life, these shattering experiences of betrayal and fear wouldn't happen. It takes *all of us* to put Lovescaping's pillars into practice since none of this works if it's only one-sided.

Practicing vulnerability strengthens relationships and allows us to authentically be seen and heard.

Love is nurtured with vulnerability.

Solidarity

Solidarity means uniting under a common goal, extending our time, support, and care to others. Displaying solidarity means fighting *with* as opposed to just *for* someone or a cause. To be solidary means to extend our hearts to others in an attempt to create a collective movement where everyone's well-being is tied to our own individual one. Lovescaping is an enormous solidarity movement, where every human being is working together to achieve our common goal of practicing love in action. Although we often overlook the importance of solidarity, it would be impossible to survive without it.

Practicing empathy and compassion leads us to solidarity. There is no turning back once we have immersed ourselves in the lives of others through our practice of empathy, and once we have overcome indifference by being compassionate: we immediately have solidarity. Think about the causes you care about... what made you care about them? How were you motivated to take action? How has solidarity helped that cause grow?

We often witness a rise in the displays of solidarity during times of crisis. Tragedies bring people together, and this is why compassion is such a powerful bonding and binding pillar: it helps us alleviate our suffering by sharing it with others. When a natural disaster strikes, for instance, we see people coming together to help each other, without stopping to ask, "What is your political association?" or "What is your faith?" or "Do you speak my language?"

Rarely have I seen such beautiful manifestations of solidarity than in crises. It is as if for a certain amount of time, everything that human beings have created to alienate and divide us from one another disappears. We are suddenly stripped of the armor of the beliefs we have constructed and our inner core is revealed: at that moment a humbling realization takes over us. We share the experience of the tragedy and realize we are all human, and we are suffering. That's it. That's all that matters at that moment, and that's enough to turn us into solidary beings.

Many of the victories we have won for humanity have been thanks to solidarity. Through the practice of solidarity, we unite to support a mission, and therein lies its strength and power. Solidarity allows us to nurture altruism and to tie the well-being of others to our very own, one of the noblest demonstrations of love.

Love is nurtured with solidarity.

Gratitude

To be grateful means to acknowledge other people's actions with kindness, to feel a sense of appreciation and thankfulness for what we are, for what we do, for what we receive and for what we have. It goes beyond saying "Thank you," to actually feeling it. When we start to acknowledge all the acts of kindness around us and to actively engage in reminding ourselves of everything that we can be grateful for, we begin to cultivate appreciation for our lives, for all the simple things that we often take for granted.

There is a short phrase in Italian that I have always loved, "*le piccole gioie quotidiane.*" It translates to "the small daily joys," (but it sounds so much better in Italian!). These seemingly simple words hold the key to happiness, I believe. We often spend most of our lives focusing on "the big things," the milestones, the rites of passages--which are important, of course--but we overlook the smaller, simple things that make up the majority of our lives. If we suddenly were to begin appreciating the little things we take for granted all the time, things like breathing, seeing the blue sky, feeling the sun's warmth, watching flowers bloom, being hugged, and, at its most obvious, *being alive,* we would live a far happier life. We are so used to all of these things, that we find them ordinary, when in fact, if we changed our lens, we would find they are quite extraordinary--beginning with the miracle of our very own existence.

Being grateful nurtures that sense of extraordinariness that makes existence special. It is almost like uncovering the world for the first time, and realizing how fortunate we are to be here. It is always possible to find something to be grateful for, and if you make it a habit to wake up every morning and find at least one thing that you are grateful for, I can guarantee your life will be infinitely more fulfilling. Expressing our gratitude to others also nurtures our relationships. When we begin to show appreciation for the things others do for us (from the small to the big), we are letting them know that their actions are meaningful, that they have an effect on us, that they matter. When you remind the people in your life that you are grateful for their existence, you validate their humanity.

Love is nurtured with gratitude.

Forgiveness

Forgiveness means being able to let go of the negative emotions that someone or something made us feel, and finding peace within ourselves to forgive others, even when they have caused us pain. The process of forgiveness is difficult and takes time. But, in the end, it benefits us, since holding on to anger, resentment, and hatred will only cause us more pain. As flawed human beings, we all make mistakes and are capable of hurting others, often times unintentionally. Being able to forgive others and asking for forgiveness are acts of love, and necessary ones if we want to nurture a relationship.

Some people view forgiveness as a sign of weakness, as an ego-shatterer, or as an "easy pass" for others to get away with their hurtful actions. If anything, forgiveness is the opposite. Asking for forgiveness is a humbling and courageous endeavor; it shows the other person that we care, that we are self-aware enough to acknowledge that we have made a mistake. The act of forgiving others is not only empowering but also liberating, since we free ourselves of the negative emotions that their actions made us feel.

There is a distinction I'd like to make between forgiving and forgetting. Forgiving helps us overcome obstacles and difficult moments, but this doesn't mean that we should "put up with" any form of abuse. There are instances where we need to forgive but not forget, so that we can move on and say enough when it is enough and not fall into a vicious cycle where we are constantly forgiving and someone else continues to hurt us. Self-love comes first, and any form of abuse is unacceptable.

Forgiveness helps us heal. As with any physical wound, emotional wounds also need time to heal. In these situations, we need to exercise our patience and allow for the necessary time to pass in order for us to experience the liberating feeling that our hearts are able to forgive. Often times, forgiveness can be a very private and intimate action, a process that takes place within ourselves. It can even become unnecessary to verbally tell the person who hurt us "I forgive you." What matters most is that internally we undergo the transformation and the liberation, and we are ready to forgive.

Love is nurtured with forgiveness.

Hope

Hope is the guiding light that carries love through difficult and dark times. Hope means having faith in humanity and in the broader goal of creating a society based on the principles of love. It means believing that things will get better, that situations will improve, that change is possible. Hope is never lost in the pursuit of love, and it is the one pillar that can never, *ever* fall in our temple. Hope is always strong, holding the structure together and allowing us to rebuild the others.

Having hope helps us survive. It is like the sun that rises every morning to remind us there is another day, a new possibility, another chance. When we go through harsh times in life, it is almost impossible to overcome them if we don't have hope. The minute hopelessness takes over our life, we suddenly lose meaning, our ability to envision a new, better tomorrow. It is a dark and scary place, and many times it doesn't end well, for what is the point of living if we don't actually see the light at the end of the tunnel? We give up. This is why, as hard as it can be to find hope at times, it is imperative that we hold on to it with all our might, because the possibility of a better tomorrow never ceases to exist. Hope exists precisely because a better tomorrow *is* possible, and we just have to remember that when we are on the verge of losing it.

Being hopeful also helps us extend and share our hope with others. If hope is a candle, and ours is ignited, we can ignite the candle of another whose light has been extinguished. Yes, hope is transmittable, and this allows us to ensure that when someone's hope is flickering and growing dim, we can come right up to them and re-ignite it. Hope is not mere wishful thinking, nor is it a delusion; it actually embodies our human potential, it exists because it represents what is conceivable, imaginable, and possible.

When I say hope helps us survive, I mean it in the most literal way possible. Having hope can be the catalyst that helps us overcome adversity. Indeed, being hopeful gives us the strength to fight, to overcome obstacles, to actually have a better tomorrow- in a way, it becomes a self-fulfilling prophecy. Love is hopeful, it never gives up, and it reveals what is possible once we let it permeate our lives.

Love is nurtured with hope.

Lovescaping in Action

Imagine a world where everyone's voice is heard, where we establish relationships and exchange love, ideas, culture, stories, and knowledge in a respectful and humble manner. Imagine a world where there is no oppression, no war. Imagine a world where dignity and respect are championed, and where different forms of knowledge are valued. Imagine a world where schools become places where we learn to love. Imagine how different our world would look if we embraced Lovescaping as a way of life.

Once, during a class discussion on Paulo Freire's *Pedagogy of the Oppressed*, one of my colleagues suddenly asked: "What is the logframe[1] of love?" A still moment of uncomfortable silence and a few giggles followed, and the class shrugged the question off, dismissing this serious, important, and central question. It might seem amusing to suppose that there could possibly be a logframe for love the same way we

---

1 Logframe is short for logical framework, and it's a tool used to plan out projects.

have logframes for planning out projects, but in fact, this question taps into the core of my work in education and my Lovescaping philosophy: we can teach people how to love.

Let us consider what Lovescaping in action would look like if we began this work in schools. I believe schools are places of transformation, where we can develop our potential as human beings who practice love in action. If we start there, the ripple effect would expand to all spheres of life. Imagine what our communities, governments, businesses, and hospitals would look like if all of us learned to love in our schools? Imagine how we would value different points of view and ideas. Imagine how we would explore multiple perspectives in order to critically think, analyze, consider, empathize, understand, and accept each other. Imagine what we could accomplish.

Our education system does very little to nurture and cultivate healthy emotions, self-value, self-esteem, or self-love. How can we practice love through our actions if we never learn to love? Imagine if schools served as safe, loving, and nurturing environments where students learned the skills that create love. Imagine what our society would look like if we incorporated Lovescaping as a core element of education, and we could develop and work on our pillars across our entire schooling journey. We spend some of the most formative years of our lives in schools, and if we were able to make use of this precious time to practice the pillars of Lovescaping, we would graduate high school with the tools to practice love in action throughout our lives.

If schools become places where we learn to play the Lovescaping symphony, where we join the pieces of our puzzle and together build our strong temple through the practice of our pillars, surely our world would enter a new era. The next generation of human beings would exemplify the pillars of Lovescaping in every aspect of their work and lives. Imagine the humanity of tomorrow, based on a system of trust and respect, where organizations are led with honesty, resolving conflicts with empathy and humility; where we are taught to forgive; where we express our concern for one another through solidarity and caring actions; where we celebrate being vulnerable; where we extend our compassion to share our suffering; where we communicate clearly and unabashedly; where we value patience as we understand that important things take time; where we practice gratitude for all the small daily joys; where our liberation is tied to each other's, and where we never lose hope and use it as a guiding light through this rocky but rewarding path called love.

I don't mean to suggest that Lovescaping should *only* be a subject we learn in school. This is not the end, but instead a powerful and impactful means by which we can lay the foundation for our next generation to be equipped with the tools to love. As adults, our habits are more difficult to un-learn. We become so set in our ways that it requires an extra-effort for us to become self-aware enough to realize where we took a detour on our road to love.

Though it may be more challenging as we get older, we all have the ability to learn and improve our Lovescaping skills at any given point in our lives. I encourage you to start by leading the way. Show love through your actions, begin today. Even the smallest acts can have enormous repercussions. Our actions are a reflection of ourselves.

The *Sentipensante* Language

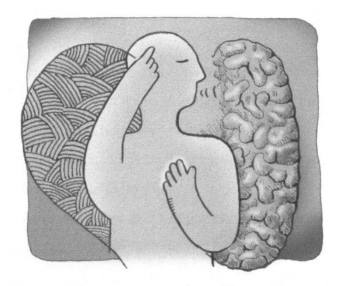

The word *sentipensante* brilliantly captures the idea of merging thoughts and feelings to describe a state of being. *Sentir* (to feel) and *pensar* (to think) are still segregated, especially in education, where we focus on the head much more than on the heart. The term *sentipensante* was originally shared by Orlando Fals Borda, one of the fathers of participatory research during his studies of communities of subsistence farmers in the coastal regions of Colombia. Sentipensante was used by the people to describe their way of life and the importance of giving equal validity to matters of the head (*razón*) and matters of the heart (*corazón*).

If we conceive of education as an opportunity to teach the sentipensante language, in which love is taught in terms of thought and feeling, we would be changing the way we think and act in all aspects of our common life. We excel at asking "What do you think?" but how about asking "How do you feel?" instead? If we could connect the heart and the mind to what the students are learning, we would be engaging them as *whole* beings and allowing them the opportunity to express all their feelings and emotions. Through the sentipensante language, we embed all pillars of Lovescaping into our lives, from the lessons we teach our children to the strategic plans we make for our lives, professions, and communities. As we do this, we give equal value to how we feel and what we think.

By acknowledging the importance (and recognizing the lack) of love in education, and more broadly in society, we open a channel for the possibility of establishing Lovescaping as our new paradigm. Lovescaping as a way of life entails a constant striving towards ensuring that we are all embraced: because if one person is in shackles, we are all in shackles. This way of life allows us to develop a social conscience that makes us more aware of our neighbors' needs and allows us to live in harmony within our community where our collective meaning and reality are shared through a "we:" uBuntu. It also allows us to constantly be engaged in the practice of learning to love ourselves, since we cannot teach others how to love if we don't practice self-love.

In *Teaching to Transgress,* bell hooks highlights the importance of well-being: "Progressive, holistic education, 'engaged pedagogy'... emphasizes well-being. That means that teachers must be actively committed to a process of self-actualization that promotes their own well-being if they are to teach in a manner that empowers students."

A self-actualized individual must be self-loving, and therefore capable of loving others. Thich Nhat Hanh, the Vietnamese Buddhist monk who has greatly informed hooks' work, emphasizes that "the practice of a healer, therapist, teacher, or any helping professional should be directed toward his or herself first, because if the helper is unhappy he or she cannot help many people." The concept of a "helping professional," and of the teacher who helps her students on the path to self-love can be problematic if not explained properly.

Murri artist, educator, activist, and academic Lilla Watson offers the right approach to envision this collective chain of help in which the helped is not dominated by the helper: "If you have come here to help me, you are wasting your time, but if you have come here because your liberation is bound up with mine, then let us work together." Notice how there is no hierarchy, no power dynamic under this paradigm; instead, there is an implicit solidarity, an intrinsic interdependence and interconnectedness in which your well-being, your freedom, and your humanity is inevitably bound to mine.

In his 1925 essay "What I Believe," Bertrand Russell claimed, "The good life is one inspired by love and guided by knowledge." I couldn't agree more with this statement. Russell goes on to say, "Although both love and knowledge are necessary, love is in a sense more fundamental, since it will lead intelligent people to seek knowledge, in order to find out how to benefit those whom they love." In an education guided by the pillars of Lovescaping, knowledge is co-constructed by the educators and the learners. Every learner brings to the table a new and different way of observing, of thinking, of knowing, and of existing in the world. How do we give value and voice to their experiences? How do we connect the curricula to their past, present, and future? How can we make it relevant and pertinent?

Unfortunately, love is not a core part of our education system, partly because it is not defined and partly because it cannot be measured--if it cannot be measured, it does not exist, right? The measurement frenzy that has taken over our schools greatly undermines the importance of love and of the social and emotional skills that we need in order to be equipped to face the challenges of a globalized, polarized, and divided world. Evidently, there is not a single magic instrument that can measure love in its entirety.

But if we were to use a comprehensive and holistic approach to measuring, meaning not just using quantitative data, but also qualitative information based on people's lived experiences and changes undergone, we can start observing the crucial role that love plays, not only in our educational experience but also in our human experience. And the results will be so telling that they will represent a truly revolutionary change in our history. We will witness a decrease in conflict, inequality, war, and in most problems that plague our world.

Sometimes I feel defeated because our education systems so often discourage this sort of philosophy. In a standardized model of education tied to high-stakes testing, there is little room for creativity, for questioning, problem-solving, or thinking outside the box. Educators are evaluated on how well their students can perform in these standardized tests and end up having to teach to the test, which is the exact opposite of co-constructing, exploring, and thinking creatively. We need to change the system, but in order to do so we must all come together and acknowledge that there is something fundamentally wrong with our current model. What are we educating our children *for*? What are the skills and knowledge that they need to be prepared to face the challenges of our globalized twenty-first century world?

The answer to this question is tricky because technology is advancing so rapidly that it is challenging to keep up with the changes. Though the path is not clear or easy, in order to move forward, we must equip our children with the social and emotional skills to learn to work together, problem solve, think creatively, and determine solutions.

The questions they will need to solve do not have a simple right or wrong answer as in a standardized test. The questions they will face throughout their lives are open-ended, evolving, thorny, messy, and multi-faceted. As our communities become increasingly diverse, our world more complex, and our problems more global, it is imperative that we learn how to cooperate, how to live in peace with one another, how to be solidary, how to care, and how to empathize and understand others who are very different from us. In other words, we need to learn how to Lovescape in order to ensure a better future for generations to come.

Teaching to Love. Finding meaning.

For me as an educator, it is in my students' actions, experiences, letters, poems and feedback that I find meaning. Teaching for me has always been first and foremost about love: both about teaching students how to *love* themselves and how to *love* each other and me *loving* my students, and about instilling in them a *love* for learning. In the process, I have witnessed the blossoming of my students, the infinite possibilities that arise once they believe in themselves--once they cultivate their self-esteem, their self-value, and, most of all, their self-love.

This is why I know that schools can be transformative. I have always made my classroom a liberating space, where each one of us (and I say "us" because it is not a hierarchical relationship--I am as much a learner as a teacher) has the freedom to explore. Together, we explore meaningful ways of being in the world, of expression, of thinking, of writing, of singing, of dancing, of living. In celebrating all the differences that make us unique, we share the most important uniting force: as individuals and as a group, we love. We love through validating our opinions, our self-expression, and our uniqueness--without prejudice and without fear.

What is it that makes a classroom a special place where love can be nurtured, taught, learned, and practiced? What does love in action look like? I started doing research, reading essays and dissertations from educators who struggled with similar issues. A lot of their work resonated with me, with many of the feelings I have towards education, the world... Yes, I found solace, inspiration and hope in bell hooks, in Paulo Freire. Yes, in other many brilliant minds that I admire. But suddenly I stopped. I realized I was looking in the wrong place. Not because these educators' ideas or techniques were wrong or because I did not agree with them, but instead because I felt that as much as I appreciated what I was reading, I could not connect with it. It was outside. I was conducting an external search for something internal that I have carried with me ever since I can remember. I was not looking in the right place.

What am I doing? I thought to myself. It is not in academic research where I will find what I am trying to bring forth, to share, to do. As I read through my students' work, their letters, poems, and feedback to me, I reconnected to the meaning of it all, to my passion, my purpose.

There, right before my eyes, lay the evidence, the proof as to why education cannot be *but* a profession of love. *Why do I have such a strong conviction that this is true, that this works?* Where is my evidence, my qualitative and quantitative research that proves that my methodology--what I have since come to term Lovescaping--works?

It took me a long time to name what I was doing, what I wanted to do: I wanted to love, to transmit that love, and to use love as the guiding force for teaching anything, from a language, to a complex biological concept, or even a mathematical formula. And if I allowed our classroom to be the place where we utilized our potential as human beings capable of loving ourselves, one another, and the world around us, I could do that.

Where do we even begin? I ask myself every day when I think of our world with all its problems. I choose to start here, with love. Love is the beginning, the means, and the end.

We need schools to be sites where we can all develop the tools and the skills to learn how to love. We need children educated in love to grow into positions of responsibility in our world. We need remedial work in love for all those who were raised in a system based on fear rather than on love.

As I looked at the evidence before me, piles of papers with my students' words written on them, journals that I have kept throughout the years, I regained hope and I found meaning. It was there, right in front of my eyes, the words I needed to name this methodology, this philosophy, this way of life, of practicing education: it was love, love in action.

What are the qualities of the educator and the class environment that make it the ideal place to nurture love? My experience so far as a Lovescaper and an educator gives me the following framework through which I continue to explore and develop Lovescaping as a philosophy and a way of living and teaching. I read and took note of all the feedback that I have received from my students, colleagues, mentors, teachers, friends, and family throughout my life, and I started coding the themes and words that appeared over and over in their writing to me, from the very young to the very old. I found recurring concepts that help me validate Lovescaping. They are:

Having an open heart and embracing everyone

Fighting for peace, justice, and reconciliation

Having integrity

Total submission/dedication

Being generous

Being unconditional

Being non-judgmental

Being passionate

Building self-confidence

Nurturing inspiration

Finding the good and the best in others

Finding beauty everywhere

Being joyful and happy: showing pleasure and
delight in teaching

Being kind and friendly

Being vulnerable, open, honest, caring

Being humble

Being patient

Sharing: coexisting, collaborating

Being considered and treated equally

Being accepting

Being respectful

Being lovable

Being genuine

Being courageous

Being empathic

Creating a vision

Bringing light

Establishing trust

Bringing Light

The reference to bringing light in the classroom that my students mention takes me back to Dr. Martin Luther King Jr.: "Darkness cannot remove darkness, only light can do that." In several of their notes to me, my students mention transitioning from darkness to light. "You have given us the opportunity to leave darkness and enter clarity," reads one, and another says, "You are a light that guided my steps because since then I had reason to progress."

Students who are treated with love realize that anything is possible, that they can have a vision, and that through our numerous conversations, dialogues, sharing, and collaborations, they are able to see light. Igniting that flame is crucial in our classes if we want our students to believe in themselves and want to show them that we believe in them. Hope contributes to keeping them motivated. That journey of transitioning from darkness to light serves as the perfect metaphor for education as a whole and love is a guiding light in that journey.

Creating a Vision

Having a vision is linked to the previous idea of transitioning from darkness to light and bringing light to the classroom and to the student's life. This light ultimately translates to having hope. I have worked with many students for whom the past indeed does not generate hope. A past that is stricken with grief, loss, war, and oppression offers very little room for hope. Hope can only exist for the student when there is a vision for a brighter future ahead; and that brighter future becomes possible when the teacher opens that door of possibilities through the cultivation of love and knowledge--love being the medium through which it becomes possible to acquire knowledge that leads to learning a skill that can be used to create a vision for a better tomorrow. This action requires the participation and the support of the entire class. Hope is contagious, and when the student realizes that she is not alone in this struggle, it becomes even stronger, the vision becomes clearer when everyone is striving towards it. The teacher's love can be the catalyst for the students' vision to start taking shape and to begin hoping and envisioning collectively. As Paulo Freire so wisely said, "The struggle for hope is permanent, and it becomes intensified when one realizes it is not a solitary struggle."

Acceptance and Congruence

Lovescaping is based on the premise that we practice what we preach. Essentially, this means being congruent, that our actions match our words. Congruence is what binds theory and practice together, and love cannot exist when there is no congruence between the two. My students' reference to being accepting refers to the ability to listen to and accept different views. Acceptance is tied to humility, since we cannot learn to accept if we are not humble enough to recognize our own limitations and to understand that none of us possesses the ultimate truth. Empathy also helps us develop acceptance, since being able to place ourselves in other people's shoes allows us to see the world through their lenses and feel with them. When we do this, it is easier to understand their views, even if they do not match ours. Being accepting also leads to transformation, since the person we are practicing acceptance with feels respected and validated and therefore can open up to becoming accepting with us--a cycle which ultimately leads to our embracing each other.

My classes, both in formal school settings and in informal ones—gatherings of friends, an outdoor picnic, or anywhere I see the teachable moment--are spaces of discovery, curiosity, and freedom, where I learn as much as, or more than, my students. The curriculum we use is a work in progress: we create it as we go, adapting it to the needs and interests of the students. It is a process of co-creation. I encourage my students to be creative and to take ownership and feel proud of their work. We explore different ways of expression, whether that is in a form of a song that they wrote to sing out in class, or a poem, a dance, a painting... Their creative work inspires me and makes me feel proud of them and privileged that they have chosen to share it with all of us in the class. The students share and participate because they feel valued and validated. I always encourage and support them, and I make sure that the others do so as well. Love then begins to be nurtured collectively through the support and admiration of the work that each one of us is able to produce.

Learning occurs when the educator has built a loving environment and a loving relationship with her students. Very early on I realized the powerful effect that teachers had on me at school. Those who live on in my heart and my memory are those who loved me. As I have said, at its core, education cannot be but a profession of love; and therefore, all of us, especially those in teaching roles, have the first, most important, and most difficult task: to learn to love. If the educator learns to love himself, his students, his mission, his subject, and his task, he will succeed in teaching the students.

Teaching is an act of love, it is a practice, and through our example as Lovescapers, we can serve as the embodiment of love in action-- and what better way to teach than through example? I have come to realize that my certainty in love as the essential condition of education is deeply rooted in my experience teaching as an act of love. That subsequently evolved into not just teaching as an act of love, but teaching *to* love. And this is what Lovescaping is about--I turned inward to my experience, to my students' and communities' voices to find the evidence that what I have shared with you here exists in practice, it works, and it yields incredible results: human beings turn into Lovescapers.

Hope: The Standing Pillar

I know I am not alone in this pursuit and in this belief that love is the single most important expression, experience and purpose of humanity. Dr. Martin Luther King Jr. has been a constant source of inspiration and hope, and it is rare to find such powerful, true and profound words and acts of love as the ones he spoke and lived: "I have also decided to stick with love, for I know that love is ultimately the only answer to mankind's problems." Dr. King's description of agape, a Greek principle for unselfish and altruistic love, resonates with Lovescaping. King explains agape as:

...disinterested love. It is love in which the individual seeks not his/her own good, but the good of his/her neighbor. Agape does not begin by discriminating between worthy and unworthy people, or any qualities people possess. It begins by loving others for their sakes... It springs from the need of the other person... It is love in action. It is love seeking to preserve and create community. It is insistent on community even when one seeks to break. It is a willingness to sacrifice in the interest of mutuality and a willingness to go to any length to restore community...

Agape demands intentionality as much as Lovescaping does. It is a constant pursuit, a willingness, an action. The pursuit and insistence on community is aligned with uBuntu, and love serves as the vehicle by which community is obtained and attained, above all else. Love in action is precisely what Lovescaping entails, and through the constant practice and renovation of the pillars of love in our daily actions, we live in a manner that is congruent, where theory exists only because it is practicable. Paulo Freire in his introduction to *Pedagogy of the Oppressed*, states: "From these pages I hope at least the following will endure: my trust in the people, and my faith in men and women, and in the creation of a world in which it will be easier to love."

The contemplative physicist Arthur Zajonc and the art historian Joel Upton have taught a course called Eros and Insight at Amherst College that attempts to explore the relations between love, knowledge and contemplation. In his deeply moving essay "Love and Knowledge: Recovering the Heart of Learning through Contemplation," Dr. Zajonc takes on the challenge of bridging knowledge and love: "I would like to add another element, one that is extremely difficult to speak of within the academy, yet which I feel is central to its work, namely the relationship between knowledge (which we excel at) and love (which we neglect)." Dr. Zajonc voices the same criticism that many others and I express about academia:

The curricula offered by our institutions of higher education have largely neglected this central, if profoundly difficult task of learning to love, which is also the task of learning to live in true peace and harmony with others and with nature. We are well-practiced at educating the mind for critical reasoning, critical writing, and critical speaking, as well as for scientific and quantitative analysis. But is this sufficient? In a world beset with conflicts, internal as well as external, isn't it of equal if not greater importance to balance the sharpening of our intellects with the systematic cultivation of our hearts? Do not the uses of social justice, the environment, and peace and education all demand greater attention and a more central place in our universities and colleges? Yes, certainly...

The systematic cultivation of our hearts. The first time I read those words I could not carry on reading. I read, re-read, underlined, highlighted, and wrote them on my journal. They became a sort of mantra that I would whisper to myself over and over. Dr. Zajonc had expressed in a simple phrase such a profound idea that made it all come together for me. I want to systematically cultivate the hearts of all my fellow human beings through the practice of Lovescaping.

Dr. Zajonc outlines the curriculum they used in the class that very much focused on building love, trust, community through respect, gentleness, intimacy, participation, vulnerability, transformation, formation, and insight. Both self-love and love of others are central tenets of the course. The results are inspiring, for students undergo a true awakening that leads them to love. In the final assignment students are asked to re-imagine their education in light of eros and insight. One of the student's responses illustrates the depth of the course in his life as he exclaims: "How do I tell them [his parents] that now the only thing that I want to be in life is a lover?"

Practicing Lovescaping is a continuous actualization, a constant pursuit; it is not a target we reach and therefore we can stop and retire. The actualization of love is a lifelong commitment, a work in progress, and we can always get better at it. As a Lovescaper, I practice Lovescaping every day of my life, in all of my actions, from the smallest and seemingly trivial to the biggest and seemingly most important--this is where the real work is done, out in the world, interacting with people on many capacities all the time.

There is no better way to teach a concept than through example, by leading the way. It is through our actions that we will actualize Lovescaping; and in this intentional endeavor of attempting the most difficult task of all, I have also started teaching my Lovescaping class.

It consists of a curriculum that teaches the fifteen pillars through a series of activities that include games, role play, discussions, circles, reflection, and artistic creation, to engage the students through the sentipensante language. I started my first pilot projects where I'm currently living, in Houston, Texas, USA, at different public schools, working with children and adolescents during the school day. Even though the programs are in early stages, the students have been very receptive to the classes, especially because they represent a space where we can explore real human connection. It is so clear that there is nothing they want more than that. We have been learning to walk in other's shoes (literally) in order to metaphorically understand what empathy is all about. We have been creating works of art to remind ourselves of all the things we are grateful for. We have been sharing all the ways in which we show that we care about ourselves and others. We have been practicing our communication skills through role play, and learning to trust one another with games that require us to blindly rely on each other. We have been Lovescaping together, and this is only the beginning of this systematic cultivation of our hearts.

But can you imagine if we could incorporate Lovescaping into our core curricula across the world? The same way we have math class, reading class, history class, we would also have Lovescaping class, where we can collectively learn how to love. I want to teach Lovescaping across the world, to human beings of all ages, to go through all the pillars one by one, understand what each one means, and learn how to practice them. I look forward to expanding this lifelong dream, to intentionally teach how to love, and I encourage each of you to Lovescape with all your actions, and to teach the pillars to the people around you, so that they may learn and in turn, teach it to others. This way, we can build a virtuous chain where love becomes the means and the end of our human experience.

***

A month before leaving Mozambique, Elias gave me a pocket planner with quotes from leaders, thinkers, artists and philosophers from around the world. All the quotes resonated with me, in particular the very first one, a quote by Eleanor Roosevelt, which Elias had underlined for me: "*One's philosophy is not best expressed in words; it is expressed in the choices one makes. In the long run, we shape our lives and we shape ourselves. The process never ends until we die. And, the choices we make are ultimately our own responsibility.*"

This is how I choose to remember Elias, singing and playing his guitar, with that *joie de vivre* that he so contagiously shared with the world. And Lovescaping is how I choose to live my life. Fellow Lovescaper, may our actions and choices reflect the pillars of Lovescaping and may we carry them out with great responsibility.

Epilogue

The Fight Against Cynicism

In this world we live in, it's far easier to be cynical than it is to be hopeful. Recall that at the beginning of this book, I gave the example of the two roads, the blue one and the yellow one. Being cynical is like taking the blue road: it almost excuses us for giving up, since there is no point in fighting for anything. Cynicism is very tempting; we are constantly bombarded with bad news, and we stand witness to all the acts that are the antithesis of love every day around the world. Yes, there are multiple reasons to become cynical, to lose hope in humanity, to despair of the possibility of a loving society. But I refuse to take this road, and in doing so, I am actively choosing love over cynicism, and fighting every day against it. It is a conscious, purposeful, and intentional choice--just as practicing Lovescaping is. I encourage you to hold on to hope and to refrain from turning a blind eye--cynicism is an excuse for inaction and we must fight vigorously against it.

Rise Above

Lovescaping is by no means easy work, especially because we live in times of great polarization and fear. We are starting this work on uneven playing fields, and this further contributes to the difficulty in actualizing a love-driven society. It is up to each one of us to choose to enact our part as Lovescapers. It is no excuse to say, "Others are not doing it, so why should I?" Imagine what the world would look like if we all lived by this mantra.

In order to start this work, we must rise above hatred, rise above fear, rise above oppression, rise above violence, rise above racism, rise above all the antitheses of love, and, instead, blaze the trail for Lovescaping. It is up to each one of us to perpetuate the status quo or to lead the way to love. Whenever you are challenged, faced with one of these obstacles, remind yourself: *rise above, rise above, rise above.*

Faith in Humanity

Sometimes I do not feel like a Lovescaper. Sometimes I, too, am afraid it is all unrealistic, idealistic, or--even worse--impossible to achieve. In these moments, I fear there are too many structural issues in the world that need to be solved before we can Lovescape. I am keenly aware of the fact that for the many people struggling to find water and food, shelter, and protection, Lovescaping seems not pertinent and not a priority. But then I take a deep breath and call on hope. I remember that if we truly embrace Lovescaping as a society and live guided by the pillars of love, there will not be people struggling for water and food, shelter, and protection. A society that practices Lovescaping cannot accept rampant inequality, and will do everything necessary to provide the conditions in which entire communities can flourish.

"You understand that there's always going to be 'haves' and 'have-nots,' right?" a friend asked me the other day as I told him about Lovescaping.

My answer was, "No, I refuse to believe that. If we build a society based on the core principles of love and practice Lovescaping as a way of life, there will never be 'have-nots.' We will be living in a society of *Lovescapers,* and that will change the world."

"You have too much faith in humanity," was his response.

Maybe he is right, and maybe he is not. But I choose to see humanity through Tuti's or Elias' eyes, rather than this friend's. I will not let his cynicism impede me from following through with what I deem as the most important movement of our times: Lovescaping.

In an ever increasing globalized and polarized world, a need for an education that nurtures and teaches how to cultivate love, humility, solidarity, and respect, and that helps develop critical thinking, empathy, passion, and compassion, is not only important, but *necessary*. It is the only source of hope we have left as we embark upon the challenge of dealing with conflict and the de-humanization of the world.

Education needs to serve a broader goal for all students and for the future of the world with all its multifold diversity, with an emphasis on collaboration and co-creation. If we can make love central to our undertaking of education, development, and ways of life, then poverty and violence can be eradicated so an egalitarian society that lives in peace equipped with the tools to overcome injustices can flourish.

Our world needs much healing. Let us systematically cultivate our hearts with love.

I choose to start with Lovescaping.

Will you join me?

Acknowledgements

This book is the result of all the interactions I have had with thousands of people throughout my life. There would never be enough space to accurately write down each and every one of those people who have made Lovescaping possible. But I trust that all of you know who you are, and I don't need to name you in order for you to feel my gratitude. This work exists because of you. There are however, a few people I have to name who helped me get this book to its present state.

To my mentor, John Rasmuson: thank you for following and supporting my journey ever since I graduated from high school. Thank you for reading the very first draft of this book and providing me with valuable feedback. Your wisdom has always been a source of inspiration to me.

To my friend, Christian Kochon: it was thanks to you that I was able to name Lovescaping. Thank you for always giving me the little push I have needed to get to the next level. I look forward to continuing Dreamscaping and Lovescaping together.

To Lucy Chambers: thank you for editing and polishing my manuscript. Thank you for believing in and supporting my work.

To Domingo Oropeza: *gracias por transmitir a través de tus hermosas ilustraciones mis conceptos. Le diste vida a mis ideas, y fue un verdadero placer trabajar en equipo.*

To my friend, Kat Moss: thank you for designing my Lovescaping logo; you captured what I envisioned with so much beauty and simplicity.

To my friend, Brandie Mask: thank you for inspiring me to take my leap of faith and pursue Lovescaping.

To my friend, Stephanie Coleman: thank you for always expanding my mind and helping me dream bigger.

To my friend, José Cossa: thank you for your unwavering support of my work and giving me hope. *uBuntu. Khanimambo.*

To my dear sister, Sofía Greaves: thank you for helping me get my book to the publishing phase. I couldn't have done it without your help. *Te adoro.*

To my family: I don't think I would have been able to Lovescape had it not been for all the love you gave me growing up. You all planted the seeds in me from the moment I was born, and those seeds have grown and blossomed into Lovescaping. Mami, Mamajose, Papi, Tuti, Sofi, Tíos: *Gracias por su amor incondicional, por motivarme, apoyarme y ser fuente de inspiración siempre. Gracias por haberme dado las herramientas para ser feliz y para aprender a amar. Los amo.*

To my husband: thank you for believing in me and supporting me from the very beginning. Thank you for Lovescaping with me every day; your love is liberating.

Notes

Empathy

- Definition of empathy: Carl Rogers, *A Way of Being* (Boston: Houghton Mifflin, 1980), p.140.

The *Sentipensante* Language

- Importance of well-being: bell hooks, *Teaching to Transgress* (New York: Routledge, 1994), p.15.

- Thich Nhat Hanh quoted in: bell hooks, *Teaching to Transgress* (New York: Routledge, 1994), p.15.

- Bertrand Russell, What I Believe (New York: E.P. Dutton & Co., 1925), p.20, 25.

Hope: The Standing Pillar

- Agape: Martin Luther King, Jr. *An Experiment in Love* (1958).

- Eros and Insight: Arthur Zajonc, *Love and Knowledge: Recovering the Heart of Learning Through Contemplation.* Teachers College Record Volume 108 Number 9, 2006, p. 1742-1759 http://www.tcrecord.org ID Number: 1267

Sources

- Baron-Cohen, S. (2011). *Zero degrees of empathy* (1st ed.). London: Allen Lane.

- Brown, R. (2012). The Power of Vulnerability [Audiobook Kindle Fire Version]. Retrieved from Amazon.com

- Freire, P. (2000). *Pedagogy of the Heart*. New York: Continuum.

- Freire, P. (2005). *Pedagogy of the Oppressed*. New York: Continuum.

- Gallegos, R. (2013). *Holistic Education: Pedagogy of Universal Love*. Guadalajara: Fundación Ramón Gallegos.

- hooks, b. (2000). *All about love*. New York: William Morrow.

- hooks, b. (2006). *Outlaw Culture: Resisting Representation*. New York: Routledge.

- King, Jr., M. (1957). *"Loving Your Enemies," Sermon Delivered at Dexter Avenue Baptist Church**.* Kingencyclopedia.stanford.edu. Retrieved from http://kingencyclopedia.stanford.edu/encyclopedia/docume ntsentry/doc_loving_your_enemies/

- King, Jr., M. (1967). "Where Do We Go From Here?," Delivered at the 11th Annual SCLC Convention | The Martin

Luther King, Jr., Research and Education Institute. Kinginstitute.stanford.edu. Retrieved from https://kinginstitute.stanford.edu/king-papers/documents/where-do-we-go-here-delivered-11th-annual-sclc-convention

- Marshall, S. (2013). Thoughts on Teaching as a Practice of Love. JAEPL, Volume 19, Winter 2013-2014, 94-107.

Rilke, R.M. (2000). *Letters to a Young Poet*. Novato, CA: New World Library.